THE GIFTS I NEVER KNEW I HAD

Reflections on Ordinary Treasures

TANYA LYONS

Printed in the United States of America

Scriptures marked NASB are taken from the NEW AMERICAN STANDARD BIBLE®, Copyright © 1960,1962,1963,1968,1971,1972,1973,1975,1977,1995 by The Lockman Foundation. Used by permission.

Scripture quotations marked MSG are taken from *THE MESSAGE*, copyright © 1993, 2002, 2018 by Eugene H. Peterson. Used by permission of NavPress. All rights reserved. Represented by Tyndale House Publishers, Inc.

Scriptures marked NIV are taken from THE HOLY BIBLE, NEW INTERNATIONAL VERSION®, NIV® Copyright © 1973, 1978, 1984, 2011 by Biblica, Inc.® Used by permission. All rights reserved worldwide.

First Printing, 2019

ISBN 978-1-9162409-0-2

ISBN 978-1-9162409-1-9 (ebook)

Tanya Lyons Publishing

www.facebook.com/TanyaLyonsAuthor

Your talent is God's gift to you. What you do with it is your gift back to God.

Leo Buscaglia

Contents

Introduction

I went through a phase in childhood when I was terrified of kidnappers. I must have watched a movie too scary for me. I spent many nights straining to hear the sounds of far-off foot-steps and got very skilled at looking over my shoulder as I walked home from school. As I got older, the fear of being kidnapped was replaced by the more sophisticated but harder to articulate fear of not having enough. I became convinced I would never have adequate time, money, love, friends, posses-sions, or choices to meet my needs. I would always be without.

When you're afraid of not having enough, it's impossible to be generous. Tiny seeds of fear grow into a huge crop of insecurity. You can't enjoy what you have today because your energy is spent preparing for what could go wrong tomorrow. Even a glass that's nearly full is still five or eight or eleven percent empty. Every interaction and relationship is measured by how it will help you reach your objective, and whatever doesn't help you get what you need is a waste of time.

How I developed a mindset of scarcity is a mystery to me. My early years were spent in a place of plenty; I had clean clothes, healthy food, a nice bedroom with CareBear™ sheets, skating lessons, and spending money for Slurpee's and bubble gum. My fear was psychological, not actual; yet fear stole a great deal from me.

My journey to see the world differently is the topic of this book. Traveling from fear to hope has been slow going. It takes time to reshape the way you look at the world. First there must be a softening and a loosening of deep-rooted assumptions. Next you need courage and space to unearth those thoughts and ideas and look at them in the light of day. Finally, there's surrender: letting yourself consider, *perhaps I'm wrong; perhaps these ideas aren't absolute; perhaps there are better options.*

One of my core beliefs—"I'm in this by myself"—led to massive amounts of stress, fear, and self-protection. For if I'm on my own, there's no place to rest. If I'm on my own, the world is full of danger. If I'm on my own, there are no gifts to be enjoyed, only obligations to be met. I worked hard to be strong and independent, and these efforts reinforced the lie that I was alone. But eventually I realized I'd been wrong about many things. I wasn't carrying the weight of everything alone. God was involved in my life; He was showering me with gifts, and it was the defenses I'd built to protect myself that clouded my ability to see His care.

It was not an easy shift to make; old habits die hard. If I were to accept God's gifts and acknowledge His activity in my life, I had to surrender the idea that I was alone. But *alone* had been my comfort zone. If I was to accept His gifts, I had to surrender my stubborn independence and be willing to receive that which I couldn't repay. It sounded frightening, yet a world full of gifts speaks of a world filled with love and purpose. A world full of gifts points to a world made by a Giver, and that's the kind of world in which I want to dwell.

And so the learning began. I discovered I had a very

narrow picture of what gifts looked like. I expected boxes with ribbon, silver platters, gift cards, and delivery trucks. Little did I know there were gifts which called for effort and participation. God is more interested in helping me become loving, generous, wise, courageous, and hopeful than in passing out objects that gather dust on a shelf. Some of His gifts are designed to teach me something, shape me somehow, and strengthen me on the inside. These gifts ask something from me, and they give back more than they take.

When God gives a gift, I've learned to say *thank you* and then ask, "What am I to do with what I've been given?" God doesn't want to spoon-feed me forever. He hopes I'll become a person who creates good things, gives to others, shares what I have, multiplies my blessings for the sake of others, and deeply enjoys them myself. He loves to give, and He knows how great it feels to be able to give. For that reason some of His best gifts are ones which enable us to be gift-givers, too. Gifts like responsibility, limitations, complex emotions, and choices help us become strong, overcome obstacles, and gain wisdom to benefit ourselves and to offer others.

To be sure, God expects more from us than I realized. He sees with utter clarity what we're capable of. He refuses do for us what we're able to do ourselves, for that would keep us weak and helpless. We've been given bodies, minds, and hearts, each with its own strength and weakness. As we care for and use what we've been given we discover there's more to us than we know. Effort and learning and growth aren't punishment—they're the gifts. Incredible gifts. Life is an opportunity to build strength, grow in love, uncover potential, and contribute to the world. God delights in drawing out our potential. Like a coach, He wants us to shine on the field. He's hard at work to wake us up to our full capacity.

I used to imagine God seated in the back row of my life's

auditorium, reading the newspaper, glancing up from time to time to criticize and find fault with my performance. But I was wrong. Creator God isn't apathetic; He's attentive and devoted, and He never misses a game. He tracks my growth and development, noticing the effort I expend. He remembers where I've come from, cheers for my successes, grieves my losses, and pictures what could be. He watches the unfolding of my personality and potential with wonder and delight. And because He sees what I'm capable of, He leaves room for growth. The gap between what He *could* do and what He *does* do isn't a sign of neglect, but of respect. His patience is not apathy[1]. He invites me to participate as a co-labourer with Him, and He makes room for my voice, my actions, my ideas, my initiative.

And so I've come to realize some of the most valuable gifts I've received are ones which require something from me. Those gifts become part of me, leave a mark on me, and help me become the person I want to be. There's a lot I could say about God's gifts of raspberries and birdsong and the *aurora borealis*, gifts which are free for the taking, but I want to focus instead on the gifts which require something of us—because these gifts can be missed or ignored, undervalued or rejected.

I invite you to join me in taking a deeper look at twenty-six gifts that come to us without wrapping, but are gifts nonetheless. While they ask something from us—hard work, patience, courage, trust, and humility—they have much to offer in return.

We've been given far more than we know.

ONE

The Gift of Being More Than One Thing

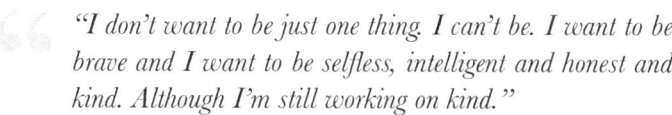 *"I don't want to be just one thing. I can't be. I want to be brave and I want to be selfless, intelligent and honest and kind. Although I'm still working on kind."*
—Four, from the film "Divergent"

We human beings are all fundamentally the same. We all belong to a common, broken humanity. We all have wounded, vulnerable hearts. Each one of us needs to feel appreciated and understood; we all need help.
—Jean Vanier, *Becoming Human*

Humans are complex and confusing and intricate and wonderful. It's hard to make sense of all we are and do. The same person can inspire one day and disappoint the next. There are people who change drastically and others who never seem to change at all. Some days my choices are golden, and other days I'm a total moron. People are complex, and trying to label anyone as *all* good or *all* bad doesn't work. Nobody has it totally right or completely wrong.

Each of us is a gloriously unpredictable mash-up of beauty and pain and potential. We're not just one thing—nor do we have to try to be. Every person alive right now is simultaneously *gifted* and *limited* and *broken,* and we will each stay that way as long as we live.[1]

What does it mean to be *gifted?* It means that God has put talent in each of us. We carry ability, potential, and strength within. Every person has something to offer. Life gives us a platform to discover, develop, and enjoy our gifts. Some gifts were simply given to us by our family or culture, without us even asking. There are other gifts we've fought for, cultivated, and discovered through immense effort. Some of our gifts are neglected or despised; some are cherished and displayed. Gifts can be stewarded or wasted, but they don't go away.

One way to look at your gifts is to learn about your strengths. In extensive research about what makes people successful, Gallup, the creator of the StrengthsFinder[2] assessment, defines strengths as something you do so naturally and so well you don't realize others struggle to do this same thing.[3] Sometimes what you're good at comes so easily you can't see it. However, most of us are painfully aware of the strengths we don't have. We focus on our weaknesses, comparing ourselves to others and wondering if we're good enough.

It's a mystery why some gifts are on the surface and others are hidden. Some gifts seem light and easy to bear, while others feel like a burden. It takes time and effort to identify and appreciate your gifts. It can be a battle to believe you're a masterpiece, created with care and given something beautiful to offer the world.

Like anything of value, our gifts require something from us. Receiving a gift doesn't mean you automatically know how to use it. Find people who celebrate your gifts, and give yourself permission to learn to use them; otherwise, they may be misunderstood or dismissed.[4] Resist the desire to compare and compete. Reject the notion that you have nothing to offer, or that you ought to be more like someone else. You are gifted. God made you that way. Your gifts are not the sum of you, but they're part of you. Your gifts are worth discovering and nurturing and celebrating. Ponder that for a while and see what happens.

Now, hold on to the idea that you're *gifted*, and think about what it means to be *limited*. Limitations are part of our design, which means there's an end to what we are. There's *you*, and then there's everything else that is *not* you. There is a start and an end to what you can accomplish, what you can understand, and what you can control. If you compare yourself to an ant, you look impressive; but next to an ocean or galaxy, you're not much to talk about. No matter how successful, healthy, or clever you may be, you remain a weak, needy creature. You enter the world with nothing and leave with nothing. Most of us eventually grow out of our dependence on others for food and clothing and shelter, but there's an inherent neediness in being human. We can't survive without sleep, food, shelter, or companionship. We require water and oxygen, encouragement and affirmation, trust and validation.

God created us with limitations on purpose. Let that sink in. We tend to resent our *limited* nature, but God doesn't see limitations as negative. They weren't an oversight. There's no shame in being limited. Our restricted capacity, say, for lifting cars, breathing underwater, or memorizing the phone book doesn't shock God. We are all limited: physically, intellectually, emotionally, and relationally. There's an end to what we can do. We can only maintain so many relationships. We must sleep. We must eat. We cannot pour out endlessly. There's a rhythm of giving and receiving to life. God invites us to rest (not just work), ask for help (instead of doing it all alone), and surrender our burdens to Him (rather than being crushed by their weight).

Limitations are a gift which invite us to connect with others, but many of us have come to see limits as shameful. We've been passed over because of what we didn't know or couldn't do. We long to be powerful and competent, to stand out because of our accomplishments. We've spent a lifetime observing the praise given to those who stand tallest and work hardest. It's difficult to believe our value can be found in something besides what we do.

While I'm warming up to the idea of limitations, they're still a hard pill to swallow. I can declare the truth *I have limits*, and *my friends have limits*, and *everyone in the world has limits*, but still be disappointed when I can't do what I want. It feels awful to say *no* to a friend simply because there's not enough of me to go around. Life with limitations is full of tension. However, as I learn to accept my limitations, I can release others from the expectation of being *un*limited. I can be kind to a friend who misjudges her time and cancels plans. I can be patient with a coworker who's learning the ropes and can't tow his weight. I can be gracious toward a leader who doesn't have the emotional energy to hear my every concern. Aren't we all doing our best to make sense of our limits?

Admitting my limits lifts a huge weight from my shoulders. God isn't angry because I *can't* do everything. Limits give me permission to accept—even ask for—help. Needing help is not a mark of failure. I don't have to do everything alone, and I don't have to control the world. I can't control weather, traffic, or the price of avocados. Purses get stolen; flights are delayed; people change their minds. The world is full of limits. Our bodies are limited, too. Migraines, infections, the flu, jet lag, and sprained ankles make it very clear we're not indestructible. We're fragile. We need care, and denial of such truths leads to more problems. But if I can accept my limits, release my urge to control the weather, people's emotions, or the price of vegetables, I have more energy to spend on what I can influence: what I say, when I go to bed, the books I read, or how often I complain. It feels good to focus my energy where it makes a difference.

So, adding the idea of being *limited* to our *giftedness*, let's make room for one more characteristic of all people: *brokenness*. Are you surprised? Me neither. Being broken means we bear the marks of life in a world far from what God intended. All of us have been touched by the influence of sin and death. We are immersed in broken families, minds, bodies, and relationships, even while we hear whispers of a future restoration.

Brokenness comes from many places. How and where we're broken varies for each of us, and we've all been wounded by circumstances, choices, mistakes, and ignorance. Some brokenness is the result of what we've done. Some is the result of what's been done to us. And whether a vase is thrown in anger, knocked over by a gust of wind, or smashed for a science experiment, it's still broken. Brokenness is not the final word, but it's real, and life in a broken world is very complicated.

How we respond to brokenness is different for each of us; it's not "one size fits all." At times we respond with anger, shame, or disappointment; at other times we respond with grief, or frustration, or sadness; at still other times with compassion and empathy. Some of what's broken can be put back together, but not all. Some restoration is quick and simple, but not all. Sometimes what's broken lasts and lasts and lasts.

Each of us are broken, but broken isn't *all* we are. The what and how of our brokenness doesn't define us. Being

broken doesn't negate our value or significance. God sees all
the parts of us: the broken, gifted, and limited parts. Brokenness doesn't disqualify us from love or restoration. God knows
what we've done and what's been done to us. He remembers
each tear and every rejection. He sees us more clearly than
anyone ever has or will, and He proclaims our true value and
worth. He alone can untangle our life, and if we let Him,
that's exactly what He hopes to do.

Understanding brokenness helps me be kind to myself and
to others. We're all in the same boat. Not all brokenness is visible, but brokenness and pain touch everyone. Brokenness
doesn't eliminate the potential for love. After all, everyone I
love and am committed to is broken. There's more to us than
what's wrong with us; in fact, our brokenness is where the best
spiritual growth begins. As Michael Yaconelli writes, "Spirituality is not about perfection; it is about connection...
Accepting the reality of our broken, flawed lives is the beginning of spirituality not because the spiritual life will remove
our flaws but because we let go of seeking perfection and,
instead, seek God, the one who is present in the tangledness
of our lives."[5] If I'm able to love those who aren't perfect,
then surely there are some who will be able to love me, too.
There's great hope for us, even in our mess. Our brokenness
doesn't have to be the loudest voice in the room. We're not
just one thing. We are broken, yes, but we are also gifted and
limited. We are complex, and in process, and full of potential,
and we are not on our own.

Our brokenness and limitations aren't an excuse for bad
behaviour or laziness. Our giftedness isn't an excuse for ego or
pride. If we cling to any of these to define us—*gifted* or *broken*
or *limited*—we miss out on the complexity of who we are. It's
possible we're blind to the best and worst parts of us, which is
why we need others to help us see more clearly.

Let's give ourselves and others permission to be a bit messy, a bit complicated, a bit surprising, and a bit more than we think we are. God has made us gifted and limited, and we've been broken. We all walk around with broken bits. We all struggle to understand our limits. We're surprised by our beauty and by our ugliness. We question what we have to offer. We fear rejection. We know shame. We've been placed in this beautiful and broken world, bearing God's image, doing the best we can with what we know. It's not easy to live in our world, and we must help each other. Today we have the chance to call out the gifts we see in others, to make allowance for limitations, to soothe the brokenness. It takes practice to hold these three truths in tension, but as we juggle them, as we keep picking up the pieces, dusting them off and trying again, we can appreciate the beautiful gift of being more than one thing.

TWO

The Gift of Being & Becoming

The reward you get from a story is always less than you thought it would be, and the work is harder than you imagined. The point of a story is never about the ending, remember. It's about your character getting molded in the hard work of the middle.
—Donald Miller, *A Million Miles in a Thousand Years*

And now, with God's help, I shall become myself.
—Søren Kierkegaard

Have you thought much about what makes a person who they are? Where does the unique *you* come from that sets you apart from everyone else? What are the essential parts of a person? What are the add-ons? Are you a collage of your name, birthdate, address, and social insurance number? How much do your family, degrees and titles, height, eye colour, or IQ make you yourself? What role do experiences, personality, relationships, accomplishments,

and failures have in molding you? If you lost all your belong-
ings, and the people who know you vanished, and you moved
to a new country, would you still be you? Is it possible to lose
yourself? Is it possible to find yourself?

It would be interesting to hear your responses to these
questions. I've looked at them from different angles, trying to
gather insight that aligns with my experience. There's still lots
to figure out, but as I've pondered the questions, I've noticed a
couple approaches to these questions, each providing pieces of
the puzzle.

One way to look at what makes a person who they are is
to see the *self* as a fixed entity, already determined and waiting
to be revealed. As Michelangelo sculpted the statue *David*, he
described the process in this way: the figure of David was
already inside the marble block, waiting to be seen, and all he
had to do was chisel away the bits that didn't belong. Some
people view the *self* like that. *Who* you are is already decided,
and your task is to *find* or *discover*. The *who* is waiting to be set
free. Life is a studio where you remove what doesn't belong
and allow the *self* to come forth.

It certainly seems that there's some truth to this. Parents
always say each child was distinct and different from other
siblings, from birth.[1] Perhaps you can trace the threads of
your passions, vocation, talents, and aptitudes all the way back
to your childhood. What you loved back then, you still love
now: art or music, mechanics or academics. You were
uniquely you long before you had a say in the matter. So, in
some way, we have always been who we are. Parker Palmer
says, "Before I can tell my life what I want to do with it, I must
listen to my life telling me who I am."[2]

However, I'm a bit uncomfortable with the premise that
our being is set in stone, waiting to be discovered. For if this is
the case, we're reduced to secondary, passive players in our

life, not main characters. In this scenario, someone else made the important decisions; the gift of *self* was designed, printed, packaged, and delivered, and all that's required of us is to unwrap it and say *thanks*.

Another perspective on the *self* describes our role as participatory. Instead of being given a pre-made self, like a meal package from the grocery store containing all the ingredients and instructions we need, we actively take part in forming and shaping who we become. The task is not simply to *be* yourself, but to *become* yourself. It might sound easy, but *becoming* requires a great deal of effort.

Both perspectives—being and becoming—acknowledge that you've been given a lot. God addresses us as His masterpieces: fine works of art, valuable creations that display His skill.[3] A masterpiece cannot say, "I did it all myself!"[4] because what you are and what you possess have been given to you from God. Gratitude is an appropriate response.

So, if life is a discovery of who you are and of who you're becoming, what does that mean for you? First of all, it means your choices matter. Your freedom matters; your actions and desires have value. The core of who you are matters to God. He's given you talents and strengths, potential and capacity. He's not abandoned you to figure life out alone, but He won't take over. Your life is His gift to you. You have a say in how you spend it. With His help, you can be and can become something incredible. You're not a lifeless puppet, but a co-creator with God, actively participating in *Project You*.

Secondly, it means you can live with hope. No matter what your life has been, no matter how you've lived or what you've experienced, your future can be different. To be human is to be mouldable. You're not locked into one way of living, doomed to be someone you don't want to be. There's hope and freedom in the ability to change and adapt. The future is not set in stone. Your destiny wasn't decided by a decision you made at sixteen, or twenty-one, or thirty. Life is created moment by moment; it builds and unfolds, decision by decision. You have plenty of time and space to discover and evaluate and adapt. Some people will say, "Don't change," or "Always stay true to yourself," and I smile. They mean well, but the thought of staying as I am forever is horrible! I'm glad I've changed. I want to keep changing.

So don't freak out. Don't worry too much about trying to *find out* who you are. You're already you—*and*, with God's help, you're becoming yourself more fully.[5] Even Michelangelo, with his claims of knowing exactly what *David* would look like, still had to pound away at the marble, one chisel stroke at a time. It took years to complete his work, and no one would deny it's a glorious masterpiece.

THREE

The Gift of Leading Yourself

You can create a relationship within yourself. You can be with yourself in a way that is loving, and present, and attuned... You can connect inward, with the relationship inside: with your body, with your thoughts... and change that to a conversation that is supportive and accepting.

—Hillary McBride, the Liturgists podcast ("Shame")

If you are not in the process of becoming the person you want to be, you are automatically engaged in becoming the person you don't want to be.

—Dale Carnegie

I don't have kids, but I know it's exhausting to care for a human, even a small one. Every babysitting gig I had as a teen was a countdown to the parents' return. If caring for a child was a heavy burden, how did I live so long with such a nonchalant approach to caring for myself? For decades

I've had to feed and shelter and entertain myself, but I haven't always appreciated what this entails.

The bottom line is: humans are high-maintenance. They need sleep, food, exercise, doctor visits, and clothes. You have to keep an eye on their mind, emotions, conscience, relationships, talents, education, hopes, and fears. You have to factor in a career, retirement fund, life insurance, voting, taxes, aging parents, and the passwords for way too many websites. Hiring a staff team to deal with it all wouldn't be overkill. Yet, for some reason, God has put every adult in charge of his or her own life. Clearly, He thinks very highly of our abilities.

In many ways the logistics of life are the easy bits. Basic necessities matter immensely, and when you don't have them, life screeches to a halt. But there's more to life than staying alive and paying bills on time. Self-leadership describes the power you have to direct your life. You're the boss. You're the key player. God put you in the driver's seat, and you don't have to wait passively for good things to fall from the sky. You get to decide what matters to you. You don't need an invitation before you take action, nor do you need permission to grow or learn or change. You've been given heart, soul, mind, and strength—how are you using them?

There's a brilliance to the design of self-leadership. Before you lead anyone else—a child, team, or company—you've had the experience of leading yourself. Before you help others reach their goals, you've learned by pursuing your own. Before you coach someone else to overcome obstacles, you've gained experience by conquering your challenges.

There've been times I wished I could return the gift of self-leadership. The idea of being responsible for my future and happiness is troubling. I'd prefer having someone to blame when things go wrong. However, even as I type this, I know it's not how I truly feel. I don't want someone to control my life and order me around. Control is worse than responsibility. I want freedom to choose and freedom to make mistakes, even if that freedom comes with a measure of risk. If God thinks I have what it takes to lead my life, I want to give it a go.

Accepting the task of leading yourself is huge, but you don't have to go it alone. You have friends and mentors, small groups, coaches and counselors who can teach and support and cheer you along the way. You're not the only one on this journey. Self-leadership is an assignment we've all been given, and it asks us to recognize our God-given worth. As author Parker Palmer says, "Self-care is never a selfish act—it is simply good stewardship of the only gift I have, the gift I was put on earth to offer to others."[1]

The way you treat yourself reflects how you truly view yourself. Are you kind to yourself in times of failure or weakness? Do you expect too much from yourself, or too little? Are you able to celebrate what makes you unique, including your limits and faults? Do you know your own story well enough to protect your tender spots and maximize your strengths? When you see your value and worth the way God does, you're better able to lead yourself with kindness, compassion, and courage.

Self-leadership is a dynamic process: never formulaic, never detached, never unbending. It requires you to pay attention to all the parts of you: your inner and outer world, and all the hopes, fears, stresses, desires, and disappointments you carry with you. When you lead yourself well, you're better able to love others. You've learned to put your oxygen mask on first, and you have resources stored up for times of need. And, as you discover more about the abundant life God offers, you're able to move toward it with strength and courage, using all you've been given to build your life into something you're proud of.[2]

FOUR

The Gift of Living in Real Time

Ideas matter. The world matters. Our lives matter, and the choices we make as we navigate our lives perhaps matter most of all.
—Lauren Myracle

"Supposing a tree fell down, Pooh, when we were underneath it?"

"Supposing it didn't," said Pooh after careful thought.

Piglet was comforted by this.
—A. A. Milne, *The House at Pooh Corner*

Surely I'm not the only person who has fantasized about jumping into my favourite TV show and joining in the action. The personalities of the characters, their lively interactions, and the importance of their mission draw me like a magnet. But the reality of my life is very different from what's on the screen. First of all, I don't have a hair and make-up department or a special effects team. I don't have a theme song or writers to provide me with witty banter. Yes, my life has the occasional poignant moment, but real life is… well, slower and less glamorous than TV.

I must admit, part of what makes TV so great is that I can observe it from the outside. I control the *play* and *pause*. When I get bored, or bothered, I skip to the next episode, or make it all disappear. Thanks to **IMDB** and Wikipedia, I can read previews and summaries of each episode. I don't have to wait or wonder what happens next. It's less risky and more enjoyable to be a spectator, especially because it's complete fiction.

In contrast to being in charge of what and when to watch on TV, real life comes at me without warning. There's no preview to my life, no cast list, no episode guide. I don't have a team to help me get my lines right. Each day begins as an improv sketch, and it keeps on rolling into tomorrow. I can't pause, I can't rewind, and no one freezes when I say "cut."

Am I the only one who struggles to stay ahead of the action? Does anyone else get confused about the plot's direction or wonder when the conflicts will be resolved? Do other people wish for better lines or a more interesting backstory? How do I know which characters will be around three seasons from now? Couldn't I watch the season finale now instead of taking each day as it comes?

But I find bits of inspiration in the fact that my life is real, not fictional. Every day, I'm given the chance to shape the world I'm in; a chance to move toward who I want to be; a chance to interact with other living, dynamic persons. The TV characters and plots I enjoy and idealize will always be fictional inventions of a screenwriter. There's no substance to these events. The stories and the friendships are an illusion— actors pretending to be people they aren't. At the end of the day, the cast and crew unplug, take their paycheque, and go home to a real life.

Meanwhile I'm in the middle of my own real life, and each day I can decide how to spend it. It can feel dull and ordinary; yet living in real time makes me the star of my life, the action hero in a real-time adventure. I can pursue my dreams, collaborate with others, embrace challenges, develop my talents, and add my voice to the mix. The lines I say aren't pre-written. The outcome of my choices is not predetermined. Life in real time is a lot wilder than any movie. What I say and do matters. I can speak up. I have space to experiment. I can learn as I go, change and adapt, alter my course. Sure, when I'm living in real time and interacting with millions of other players, I don't always get my way, but that's a special kind of gift in itself.

Living in real time keeps life interesting. It forces me to be present, as I truly am, and to take responsibility for my character. I get to shape this world—my world. While life in the real world comes with its share of stresses and questions, I'm grateful to be alive here, where life unfolds one day at a time, and where I'm part of making the world what it will be.

FIVE

The Gift of Changing Your Mind

> *Do not wait; the time will never be "just right." Start where you stand, and work with whatever tools you may have at your command, and better tools will be found as you go along.*
> —Napoleon Hill, *Think and Grow Rich*

> *If everything doesn't happen quite the way you'd like, it doesn't make too much difference, because you can fix it.*
> —Julia Child

I haven't met many people who *want* to make bad decisions. There's a lot of fear and frustration associated with decision-making, and sometimes all we know to do is cross our fingers and hope for the best. Because of the confusion and pressure connected to making wise and healthy choices, I've seen a lot of people hovering around or camping out in the *danger zone* of decision-making.

The decision-making *danger zone* includes the following ideas:

- There is only *one* right decision in a situation
- Any decision apart from the *right* one will produce failure, disappointment, and ruin
- Making the right decision will guarantee success and happiness
- The longer I wait, the better a decision will be
- Good decisions require exhaustive amounts of research
- Once a decision is made, I must stick with it, no matter what
- Changing my mind is a sign of weakness

It's hard to say exactly where these notions come from, but because they're so common, it's hard to evade the danger zone. As a result, many of us are weighted down by angst and fear about decision-making, always worried we won't do it right.

But what if we could avoid the traps of the danger zone and approach decision-making from a different angle? What if decision-making was an opportunity to learn? What if options and choices didn't bring stress but permission to experiment and discover? What if decision-making was as natural as walking, simply taking one small step after another? What if decision-making was more like a stroll through the woods—wide vistas, interesting perspectives, opportunities to pause, adjust course, or turn around—than it was like getting on a plane, where there's only one place to get on and one final destination?

When we believe making the *right* decision will produce a perfect outcome, we set ourselves up for frustration and failure. Good decisions can move us toward a desired outcome, but they can't guarantee it. We live in a world filled with variables that require us to face each day, each plan, each decision with bravery and flexibility. It takes guts and wisdom to take life as it comes. It takes humility and creativity to stay in the game as things shift around you. Adjusting your plan doesn't make you a flake; it makes you responsive and engaged.

Instead of trying to make right decisions, could you accept the premise that some of your plans will need to change? What if making a *good* decision and adjusting it as you go is just as smart as (or smarter than) trying to make the *right* decision to begin with? Adapting your plan doesn't mean it wasn't good; it simply means life is dynamic and changing. Success is a result of more than decision-making. It requires you to work hard, stay engaged, and adjust when necessary. Making one all-encompassing plan isn't going to ensure a perfect life. Instead it's the hundreds of small, less significant decisions that help you succeed or not.[1]

Giving yourself permission to change your mind lessens the fear of making bad choices. Decision-making is a skill that only improves with practice, trial, and reflection. Instead of pressuring yourself to be the expert authority, allow yourself to be a student learning something new. Don't scold yourself for what you don't know. Be curious and teachable; ask for input; adjust your plans; and start over again if things go sideways. Every problem you face and solution you devise teaches you something you can draw from in the future. Instead of seeing problems and challenges as negative, learn to welcome them as developers of creativity. And when you make a particularly awful mistake, consider it a rookie move and get back in the game.

Let's consider decision-making in a completely different way by talking shoes. Buying shoes involves trying on a few pairs and walking around the store, noticing where they rub, how they look, and which ones feel most comfortable. Nothing radical there. At some point, however, you have to decide, hand over the cash, and walk out, even if you're not entirely sure about the decision. Will you regret your choice? Would a different pair have been better?

Who knows? There's a limit to what you can discover about shoes by walking around the store. How much of your life do you want to spend looking at shoes? You've got stuff to do and people to see. There are streets to walk and trails to explore. When you remember the purpose of shoes, it brings perspective to shoe-buying. Research is great, but you eventually have to say *yes*, put the shoes on, and start walking.

The unknown is always difficult. It takes time to adjust to something new. Anxiety and doubts and questions are normal. If you can accept this and go with the flow, life will be better. No amount of planning can eliminate risk and uncertainty.

When you feel trapped in the *danger zone*, don't give up. It's hard not to freak out under the pressure of making a *right* decision, but it doesn't have to stay that way. Give yourself permission to try, discover, make mistakes, and try again. As you do so, you'll get better at decision-making and spend less time on the edge of the danger zone.

SIX

The Gift of Emotions

> *This being human is a guest house.*
> *Every morning a new arrival.*
> *A joy, a depression, a meanness,*
> *some momentary awareness comes*
> *as an unexpected visitor.*
> *Welcome and entertain them all!*
> —Rumi, "The Guest House"

Managing emotions requires a level of skill and effort that at times seems beyond me. Can you relate? Emotions can be tricky and wonderful and confusing and complicated, and they come with us wherever we go—which has pros and cons. Have you ever watched the commentary version of your favourite movie where someone talks non-stop through every scene? Emotions are a bit like that. They don't switch off just because we've had enough for one day, and surely I'm not the only one who'd like that option.

Emotions have an important job to do, and they work

hard to get our attention. You could say emotions are a type of thermometer, measuring what's going on in and around us, gathering data, and giving suggestions about how to respond. As good as their intentions may be, these messages can be confusing. Are we supposed to pay attention to every stomach flutter and elevated heartrate? When do we trust what they say, and when do we get a second opinion? Which nagging thoughts and questions can be ignored in order to sleep at night?

Emotions give us information about ourselves and the world. They're best able to help us if we listen to *all* they say, not only the parts we like to hear. As my friend Robin would comment, "Emotions aren't *good* or *bad*, they just *are*."[1] It's tempting to ignore the emotions we don't like and focus on the emotions we do like, but this doesn't help in the long run. Insisting you're happy and relaxed does not make you happy and relaxed. A thermometer stuck at 20°C is not optimistic or positive—it's *broken*. You can't control the temperature by willpower. But when you accurately measure the temperature, you can choose to build a fire or turn on the air conditioning. All of our emotions, even the ones we don't enjoy, offer us valuable data. If we shut them down, we can't benefit from their messages.

Consequentially, when we block the emotions we don't want to feel (like anger, fear, or grief), we hinder our ability to feel the ones we want to feel (like hope, love, connection, or peace). Emotions aren't something we pick from a menu. Numbing emotions can help us survive difficult situations, but it's no way to live long-term.

In contrast, being honest about our emotions allows us to receive the data they offer but not be pushed around by them. We are not our emotions. Feeling sad or bad or disappointed doesn't make us a bad person or a failure. Emotional numbness doesn't make us *spiritual*, or *holy*, or *superior*. We've been created to experience the entire spectrum of emotions—rage, delight, shame, exuberance, and more. If we're incapable of feeling all of them, we're missing out on what it means to be alive.

Emotions are a true part of us, but they don't define us. One way to remind ourselves of this is with the way we speak about our emotions. Instead of saying, "I am angry," say "I feel anger." Instead of saying "I'm miserable," try saying, "I feel miserable." For some reason, many of us equate success with how often we feel *happy* and *good*. This assumption needs to be re-evaluated, as there is a lot more to a meaningful and flourishing life than the frequency of certain emotions.[2]

Since emotions are designed to transmit information, it's a waste of time to argue with them. And it's exhausting. How successful have you been at talking yourself out of feeling hurt or sad or angry? How many times have you been able to talk yourself into feeling excited or happy, when you weren't? For me, the longer I ignore an emotion, the longer it takes to process it and move forward. Acceptance and validation serve me better than denial and rejection.

Of course, we don't have to blindly obey what our emotions tell us, either. Emotions give us part of the story, but not its entirety. They have a limited perspective, and the lenses they look through can get blurred or warped. Emotions aren't all-knowing; rather, they depend on our logic, intellect, conscience, experience, and relationships to bring balance and wisdom, so we can live well. Let your emotions do their part, but don't expect more from them than they can offer.

Here's an exercise to try: over the course of a day, do your best to name each emotion you experience.[3] Don't try to change how you feel, and don't label an emotion as *good* or *bad*. As you discover each emotion, think about where it might have come from and what it could be trying to tell you. Don't be in a hurry; simply savour the incredible variety contained in this gift. When you discover an emotion you'd normally push away, consider offering it hospitality instead. Thank this emotion for showing up, and invite it to deliver its message. For example, when feeling lonely and sad, try saying, "Hello, loneliness and sadness. I see you lingering over there. Thanks for stopping by. Why don't you have a seat and tell me what's on your mind?" You might be pleasantly surprised to hear what they have to say.

Emotions offer incredible treasures to us day after day, and stewarding them well requires skill, wisdom, and attention. Emotions enrich our lives by giving us a broad palette of ways to understand others, connect to them, and share the beauty of the life we've been given.

SEVEN

The Gift of Attraction

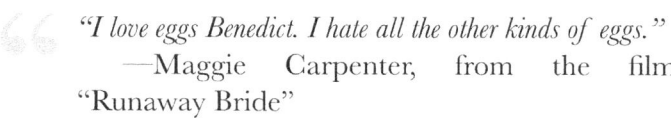

"I love eggs Benedict. I hate all the other kinds of eggs."
—Maggie Carpenter, from the film "Runaway Bride"

[T]hough I mightn't be so sure about what interested me, I was absolutely sure about what didn't...
—Albert Camus, *The Stranger*

I f *attraction* wasn't a thing, I'm not sure I'd ever get dressed or leave my house; pyjamas are incredibly comfortable. But for some perplexing reason, I'm drawn to things which require me to leave my living room. There are sunsets from the tops of mountains. Puppies. Live jazz in the park. There's swing dancing, and the smell of lilacs, and fettuccini alfredo with freshly ground pepper.

I find myself drawn to specific things and places and people in ways that don't always make sense. Is there any logic to attraction? Why bunnies, not elephants? Why blue, not purple? Why jazz, not blues; why cinnamon instead of lavender? What is this force that draws me, stirs my heart, invites me to come close?

At least attraction makes life interesting. All it takes is sunshine during a rainstorm, a wonderful Black Forest cake, or my favourite shade of blue, and a normal day is transformed into something special. No scheduling or announcement required.

Attraction is a mysterious, individualized gift.[1] The sounds and smells and tastes and places and animals and colours that bring me delight may have no impact on you whatsoever. Go figure. This is just as well, or there'd be a lot more fighting around the sale rack.

However, attraction has disappointed me more often than I'd like to admit. While attraction helps me choose what to wear each morning, narrows my vacation options, and assists with menu planning, attraction can't tell me which cars in the lot are lemons, if the beautiful watermelon will taste sweet, or if a handsome stranger will treat me with respect. Attraction doesn't measure character. It doesn't see the whole picture. When I expect attraction alone to give a definitive answer about who I date, which novels to read, or which hiking boots to buy, I will be disappointed—big time.

Attraction has a lot to offer, but in order for it to do its job, I must understand the difference between attraction and choice. Attraction is out of my control, but choice *is* in my control. Being attracted doesn't erase my obligation to choose wisely. It's possible to be attracted to one thing, yet choose something else. We all know the powerful lure of online shopping deals, the second piece of cake, or one more episode of a favourite show. We know how it feels to give in and how it feels to stay strong.

Seeing attraction as a gift has helped me be more honest about what I'm drawn to. Attraction gives me clues about how

I'm wired and what I enjoy, but attraction was never intended to make decisions for me. Not every eye-catching thing is beneficial. Not everyone I'm attracted to is available. My brokenness may pull me toward destruction, but understanding the appropriate role attraction plays in decision-making will save me a lot of grief.

Attraction is a wonderful gift. It makes life interesting and full of surprises. It adds colour and flavour to life and reflects a wildly creative God who makes each snowflake unique *just because*. So enjoy the gift of attraction for all it has to offer—which is a lot—but don't expect more from it than it was designed to give.

EIGHT

The Gift of Creativity

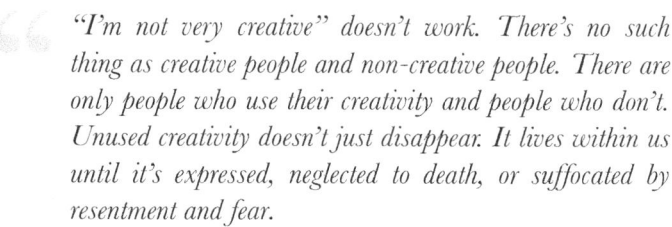

"I'm not very creative" *doesn't work. There's no such thing as creative people and non-creative people. There are only people who use their creativity and people who don't. Unused creativity doesn't just disappear. It lives within us until it's expressed, neglected to death, or suffocated by resentment and fear.*
    —Brené Brown, *The Gifts of Imperfection*

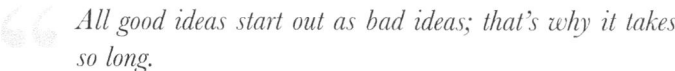

All good ideas start out as bad ideas; that's why it takes so long.
    —Steven Spielberg

If you've ever been curious, you have what it takes to be creative. Creativity and curiosity are cousins. Both of them peer below the surface, interested in what's gone before and why things are like this and what *could be* in the future. Where there's creativity, there are possibilities; there's movement and hope; and hope is a gift the world needs. Creativity invites us to consider *what if?* instead of concluding *this is how it will be.* It takes courage to ask *what if?* over and over again, but it's a skill we can cultivate.

Everyone has an imagination, and everyone can create.[1] Creativity's not reserved for certain personalities or types. Not all of us have made space for creativity in our lives, but like seeds stored in a packet, creativity can spring up when the conditions are right. Just like a seed, creativity can lay dormant for years, yet come to life with soil and water and light. The fruit of the seed, like the outworking of creativity, may look very different at the end, but it carries with it something of its source—seed or creator—with it. There's a generosity in creativity, an excitement and other-focus that wants to reach beyond. Creativity begins when the creator sees a gap between what is and what could be and takes action. There's a birthday, but no cake—why not bake one? There's an abandoned lot, empty and sad—why not sow wildflowers? Your workplace is cold and uninviting—why not rearrange the furniture and decorate? Our longing to see order, beauty, and abundance inspires action, and the results are cakes, flowers, a cozy work space, and more.[2] As we feed and water our creativity, more goodness flows from us to others.

But creativity isn't all delight and inspiration or picnics and balloons. It takes backbone and determination not to give up easily. Creativity must ignore critics and cynics. It must ruthlessly hunt for options, vigorously imagine what could be, and stubbornly take steps to make things better. If there are problems to be solved, people to be loved, or beauty to be expressed, there's a place for creativity. Creativity can feel vulnerable and uncomfortable. And why wouldn't it? You're coaxing partially formed ideas from your mind into the physical realm, and the passage always includes toil and strain. No one gets it perfect on the first try.

To create is to enter a battle over who and what is worthy to be heard. A consumer mindset is at odds with creativity. The consumer asks, *Why create when the world's already full of shows and snacks and gadgets? Why bother making something new when I can choose from what's already here?* If we believe professionals have all the good ideas, there's no need for what the rest of us offer. But what if all of us can create? What if making something new is the birthright of every human, a gift from God to each of us? What if creating isn't a competition but an invitation to bring something of yourself to the table? Your efforts and perspective and ideas are worth sharing, whether as a story or a website or a pair of mittens. Your voice deserves to be heard. And if what you have to offer is still a work in progress, please keep at it; we need what you carry inside.

Creativity can feel wasteful. Nothing makes a bigger mess than creating something new. I've spent countless hours working on ideas that didn't turn out. I've burned cakes and botched recipes. I've gone through notebook after notebook, and for what?

For the sake of learning what I didn't know and discovering the power of *what if*. Creative endeavours come with a cost. They require something from us—and it's not a waste if those hours and notebooks and awful muffins took me closer to my goal. Creativity digests every experience and perceived failure, pauses to regroup (as necessary), and formulates an alternative path. Creativity is at the heart of turning lemons into lemonade.

You don't have to be a genius to be creative. You don't need to patent an invention or record something that goes viral. Just think about what you enjoy doing and take the next step. Love reading? What about hosting a book group? Mad about trying new recipes? Why not cook through a recipe book, or make your own? Obsessed with birthday cards? Why not design some for friends? Creativity can make every email, every meal, every chat with a stranger an opportunity for blessing and connection. For if you can write for the joy of it, bake muffins for the deliciousness of it, or offer words of kindness in your particular way, you bring something of incredible value to your corner of the world, and that is a gift.

NINE

The Gift of Your Own Company

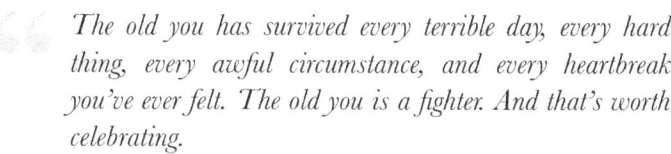

The old you has survived every terrible day, every hard thing, every awful circumstance, and every heartbreak you've ever felt. The old you is a fighter. And that's worth celebrating.
    —Emily McDowell, in "New Year's Toast to the Old You"

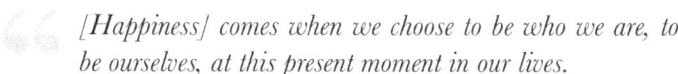

[Happiness] comes when we choose to be who we are, to be ourselves, at this present moment in our lives.
    —Jean Vanier, *Becoming Human*

Many of us have developed a bad habit of taking the people we're closest to for granted. We forget to say *please* and *thank you*. We check our phones while we talk to them. We don't laugh at their jokes. We withhold from them the kindness, respect, and courtesy we offer to strangers. It's possible to drift from familiarity to disrespect without noticing. When we take someone for granted, we stop trying to go deeper. We don't pursue; we aren't curious. We believe we know all there is to know, and it feels awful to be taken for granted.

One person it's easy to take for granted is ourselves. We're used to walking around in our own skin. Our life is ordinary, and we don't expect much. We tune out our voice like background music, critique our looks, our words, and our thoughts. We speak to and think about ourselves in ways reserved for our worst enemy. With habits like these, is it any surprise we stay busy so we don't have to be alone with ourselves? We've lost sight of how wonderful we are and what a gift it is to spend time with ourselves.

If you find it hard to appreciate yourself, look no further than your friends. For reasons unknown, they think you're fun to be with, interesting, and worthy of time and energy. Friends celebrate our victories and have compassion for our sorrows. They're curious about our ideas and dreams, and they listen to our concerns. What do they know about us that we don't know about ourselves? Perhaps it's a case of not being able to delight in what we can't see. It's possible to go through life as a stranger to ourselves, blind to the beauty and strengths we possess. So what would it look like to (re)discover the gift of our own company?

I've heard married couples say you have to keep discovering each other. You have to pay attention; ask rather than assume; and expect change and growth. It's a privilege to be married to such a complex and magnificent individual. Could you do the same with yourself? If you're not living in awe and wonder at the amazing gift of *you*, there's work to be done. After all, you're unique and incredible, unlike anyone who's ever lived. Your laugh is delightful. Your enthusiasm is contagious. Your quirks are charming. You've suffered and been pushed down, but you've gotten back up. You've loved with generosity, taken risks, and created beauty.

No one brings to the table what you bring. You're impressive.

Sometimes there's a disconnect between what we hope others will see in us and what we see in ourselves. We want people to hang out with us, but we don't enjoy our own company. What's up with that? Either we've done a great job fooling our friends about who we are, or we need to adjust the way we see ourselves.

Imagine meeting yourself for the first time. What do you notice about you? Surely there are interesting things to be curious about. What questions would you ask; what stories would you want to hear? What do you enjoy and appreciate about this person? Sure, it's a bit contrived to approach yourself this way, but it's a place to start.

Another activity which could give you a new perspective is to make a timeline of your life. Sketch out key events: moves, jobs, losses, accomplishments, and challenges. A straight line works, but so does a curvy road or a river. Who played key roles in your life at different times? What propelled you forward, and what's held you back? Where have you been stuck? Where have you leapt forward? What are some highlights and low spots? After you make your timeline, look at it again and reflect on the big picture. Where do you see growth and change? How could you describe yourself and your life? What questions do you have about where you've come from and where you want to go?

You've got tons to offer others: friendship, love, humour, support, and more. But don't neglect yourself along the way. Learn to appreciate and enjoy yourself. *Enjoy*, not just tolerate. Practice caring for and lavishing love and attention on you. Caring for yourself is a way to say *thank you* to God for the gift of you.

Learning to be a friend, cheerleader, advocate, and

companion to yourself will help you grow into the person you want to be. Don't take yourself for granted. Don't underestimate how interesting and wonderful you are; there's more to you than what's on the surface. You have a voice that's worth hearing, and being able to spend your entire life with you is a gift you don't want to waste.

TEN

The Gift of Your Yes & No

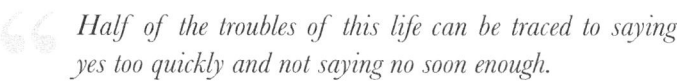

Half of the troubles of this life can be traced to saying yes too quickly and not saying no soon enough.
—Josh Billings

Compassionate people ask for what they need. They say no when they need to, and when they say yes, they mean it. They're compassionate because their boundaries keep them out of resentment.
—Brené Brown, *Rising Strong*

I don't remember learning to say "no" as a toddler, but according to parents, everything changes after that. *No* gives the child power to assert her will, reject directions, and alter the future. What other word does so much? *Yes* and *no* are two of the most important words in any language. They close and open doors to countless hopes and fears, limits and expectations, vulnerability, risk, and joy.

A two-year-old is unaware how *no* will complicate her life. Learning *no* has changed her family, and learning *no* has changed her. Deciding when to say *yes* and when to say *no* will consume a great deal of her life. These two small words require great consideration and bring about dramatic consequences.

Some of us have a habit of saying *yes* more than we ought. Some of us lean toward *no* as a default. But let's be honest and admit it's a risk to make any decision, to commit to anything. *Yes* and *no* are commitment words; they communicate what we want and care about and are willing to work for. To say *yes* or *no* is to tip over the first domino in a long line, and with one small word we launch ourselves in a direction we can't completely control, imagine, or predict.

Saying *yes* requires commitment and trust and strength. *Yes*, I'll be there when I said. *Yes*, I'll finish what I started, even when it's harder than planned. *Yes*, I'll believe my friend even when there's reason to doubt. *Yes*, I'll trust God even when I'm afraid.

Saying *no* requires courage and trust and faith, too. *No*, I won't take the easy way out, even if no one could tell. *No*, I won't yield to temptation. *No*, I won't twist the facts slightly to give myself an advantage.

Saying *yes* or *no* is scary. It's easier to say *I'm not sure*, *I'll think about it*, *You decide*, or *I don't care*. I lived in that place for a long time. I had no confidence in my choices. I felt weak and powerless. I was afraid of failure—and many other things. If I didn't decide, I couldn't fail. If someone else made the decisions, I could blame them when things went wrong. While there's logic to this approach, it gets tiring to be miserable and always blaming someone else. Letting others make all the decisions kept me in the passenger seat.

During my years of not wanting to make decisions, I still had to say *yes* and *no*. But instead of making decisions based on my wants and values, I let the needs and wants of others sway me. I'd say *yes* when I wanted to say *no*. I'd overextend myself serving, helping, being available. *Better to be stressed than lose a friend*, I'd say to myself. What I wasn't counting on was the price I'd pay for being dishonest with myself. *Yes* is a powerful word, but saying *yes* doesn't make a thing possible. Saying one thing while wanting another took a toll on me.

Being able to say *yes* or *no* puts you in the driver's seat of your life. When you're learning to drive, that seat is a terrifying place to be. There's so much to remember and so many places to look, and you can't just slam on the brakes when you're stressed. Making one mistake while driving could cost you thousands of dollars. It takes time to get comfortable with such power.

Learning to say *yes* and *no* can be terrifying, too, and it brings significant risks. But as you embrace these gifts and become familiar with them, you learn they aren't something to fear. You're not an object to be dragged around. You can disagree, go a different way, and explore unknown territory. You've been given the gift of agency, the power to decide and act; and instead of seeing *yes* and *no* as landmines about to explode, *yes* and *no* offer freedom to change your mind, redirect your course, slow down, or push pause. There are consequences to your choices, but life isn't actually a line of dominoes.

I've learnt the best *yes*es and *no*s come when I'm honest with myself and aware of God's presence with me. He is concerned with my life and will help me wield the power I've been given. Slowly and gradually, as we pay attention to our inner world and learn to trust our judgment, we find the courage to use the gift of *yes* and *no* in ways we feel good about.

ELEVEN

The Gift of a Should-Free Life

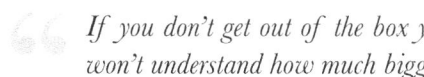

If you don't get out of the box you've been raised in, you won't understand how much bigger the world is.
—Angelina Jolie

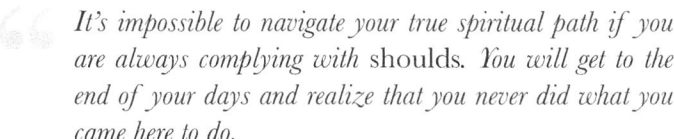

It's impossible to navigate your true spiritual path if you are always complying with shoulds. *You will get to the end of your days and realize that you never did what you came here to do.*
—Karen Kingston, "Reasons to Remove 'Should' from Your Vocabulary Forever"

S*hould* is one of those words we love to use but hate to hear. Using *should* makes me feel confident and powerful. With *should*, I hand out advice and suggestions, I convince myself which course of action is the right one, and I enjoy my lofty position as someone who knows exactly what to do. But what's more annoying than being told what I *should* do, especially if I didn't ask for advice? How does that person know what's best for me? How do they know what I'm aiming for? What arrogance.

To be fair, *should* can be helpful at certain times and in certain situations. In childhood, *should* helps us learn what's appropriate and good. It provides guidelines for kindness and consideration. These *should*s instruct and set boundaries and build habits for success in life and relationships. You *should*: be nice to your sister, eat your breakfast, say *please* and *thank you*, share your toys, listen to the teacher, brush your teeth before bed, and on and on. These are helpful suggestions, but there are always exceptions to a *should*.

If we're not paying attention, *should* switches from a useful instruction to mindless autopilot. It claims to knows what to do and what to expect in every situation. Like a type of sedative, *should* says we don't need to be attentive or responsive. If we do *this*, *that* will happen—no questions asked. *Should* doesn't want to know why or what's going on inside; it simply wants us to do as we're told.

And while *should* claims to simplify life with its rules and directives, it actually weighs us down with massive expectations. *Should* demands obedience and perfection, and it doesn't make exceptions for our limits or uniqueness. For years I struggled to be cheerful and happy and strong, but no one can be those things all the time. Why did I follow *should* for so long? Why did no one tell me there were other ways to live? As a writer, I choose written words with care, but I didn't evaluate *should*'s influence on my life. When a friend described life without *should*, I was intrigued.[1] I decided to follow suit, giving myself permission to disagree with, challenge, and ignore *should* to my heart's content.

A life without *should* took getting used to. I was happy to ignore its bossy demands, but I found myself missing its comforting guidance. I'd enjoyed the confidence *should* brings. *Should* expects cause and effect. It claims to know how things will turn out—always neat and tidy. But now, without *should*, I had to examine my motives and weigh the outcome of each choice. Why did I send thank you cards or go to church or apologize when I'd hurt someone? Were those things important to me, or were they automatic? It took more work than I expected to discover my reasons for what I did and didn't do. I had to remind myself that politeness, self-control, and thinking before I speak are expressions of love and wisdom, not arbitrary rules I keep out of fear.

At times I struggled to have normal conversation without *should*. I'd spent years passing down its rules and expectations and found it difficult to discover *should*-free ways to express my thoughts. I'd become more comfortable as an expert who gives guidance than a friend who listens. With *should* on my side, it was natural to offer advice. But without *should*, I felt less pressure to tell people what to do. Instead I could ask questions, express interest, and let people make their own decisions.

Giving up *should* increased my appreciation for the scores of amazing, intelligent people in the world. Without being ruled by *should*, there's so much I can learn. Did you know there are at least six different ways to cook rice? I used to think there was only one way—and *should* backed me up. But what I viewed as the only way is simply one of many ways. If I block out the other voices, I miss out. Getting rid of *should* lets me think harder and deeper than I did before, and it broadens my vocabulary.

Adopting a *should*-free life is an invitation to live intentionally. It takes work to make choices based on values, and it takes energy to weigh possible outcomes. Letting go of *should* doesn't mean rejecting wisdom and advice; rather, it allows us to be selective about what we listen to, whom we obey, and what we expect from the world around us. Life without *should* helps us participate in life—doing and saying what we do because we've chosen to, with eyes open—instead of being afraid to go against the whispered demands of *should*.

TWELVE

The Gift of Leaving Your Comfort Zone

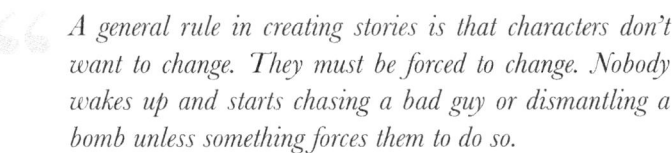

A general rule in creating stories is that characters don't want to change. They must be forced to change. Nobody wakes up and starts chasing a bad guy or dismantling a bomb unless something forces them to do so.
　—Donald Miller, *A Million Miles in a Thousand Years*

Setting out is always a leap of faith, a risk in the deepest sense of the term, and yet an adventure too. The familiar and the habitual are so falsely reassuring, and most of us make our homes there permanently.
　—Richard Rohr, *Falling Upward*

There was phase in my twenties when friends and I found it extremely entertaining to "friend-nap" people we knew and whisk them off on an adventure. Friend-napping was great for birthdays, mid-week study breaks, or as a sign of love and support after a breakup. We discovered there was something about changing location, interrupting routine, and creating shared experiences that could strengthen friendships and bring refreshment. A shift of location and circumstance helped us refocus. Getting *out* and getting *away* did wonders, and we had a blast.

In the same vein, getting out of your comfort zone (through choice or circumstance), though usually less fun, can have similar results. Leaving what's predictable and stepping (or being dragged) into unfamiliar territory is often stressful but offers renewed perspective, cherished memories, and reminders of how capable you are. Leaving your comfort zone shakes you up, clears your head, and gets things moving.

I'm the type who prefers to be prepared and in control. My purse contains items I rarely use but like to have *just in case*. I feel better, more secure and relaxed, when I have Bandaids, Tylenol, and a Sharpie with me. Even the most spontaneous of us know the sinking feeling of forgetting your phone, misplacing your wallet, or being thrown into a situation you tried to avoid.

Sometimes we boldly leave our comfort zone with determination and the courage to be vulnerable. It's exhilarating and terrifying to step into the risk-zone. Good on you for all the times you've done just that. However, it's not always up to us to decide when we leave the familiar. It's the fact we can't predict when we'll leave the comfort zone that makes it so uncomfortable. Cars break down; phones don't work; supervisors call in sick. *Leaving the comfort zone* is often a euphemism for *something really bad happening*, and that's hard.

But leaving the comfort zone is part of the natural order of things. God's been calling people to step out of the comfortable since the beginning of the human story. God asked Abram to leave his land and family and go to the place God would show him.[1] That sounds odd, and terrifying, and unexpected. And Abram did it.

A baby bird pushed out of the nest in order to fly is another example. Without the push, a fledgling would never discover the wonder of flight. The push says, *You've got what it takes, kiddo. You're strong and resourceful and not as fragile as you think you are. We believe in you.* Overwhelmed by panic and shock, the baby bird can't appreciate the affirmation; but later on, it's grateful to fly. It feels good to be believed in. Birds are supposed to leave their nests. There's nothing crazy about a creature going from one level of competence and skill to the next. We're designed to develop and change. These changes can be exciting and scary, but they help us grow. Leaving the comfort zone always comes with apprehension and fear—whether you're pushed or step out on your own. This is normal. But later on, as you look back, you see how you've grown, and you're glad for the nudges.

There are many degrees of leaving the comfort zone. It could look like going to a dance class, introducing yourself to a stranger, speaking up in a meeting, going on vacation alone, starting a job in a new field, or going back to school. It can look like moving to a new city or country, getting married, or having a child. Some departures from the comfort zone are natural and predictable; others simply feel like bad luck. The level of intensity varies, but every time you step beyond what's familiar and safe, you gain something of value.

One gift of leaving your comfort zone is what you discover about yourself. When you never depart from familiar routines and familiar roles, it's easy to stagnate; if it ain't broke, don't fix it. But leaving your comfort zone opens up the world. You could discover untapped talents or interests. I never knew I could teach until I was thrown into the classroom. You may discover you're energized by a bit more chaos, or the testing of your physical limits, or living internationally. When the pressure's on, you have to solve problems and handle stress and overcome challenges. You're creative and resourceful, and you can make it without Google. You don't wilt at the first sign of challenge; instead, you give yourself a pep talk and keep going.

When you leave your comfort zone, you discover the world is full of people who are so very different from you. Where have they been all your life? We share our common humanity, yet the variety of life experiences is vast. You would miss so much if you only see the world through the eyes of people like you. It would be like eating the same meal for breakfast, lunch, and dinner—for the rest of your life.

When you're out of your comfort zone, you're forced to ask for help. You surrender the pretense that you have it all figured out. You must embrace vulnerability and endure awkwardness. Everything takes more energy: explaining yourself, buying food, getting from place to place, completing simple tasks, making friends, making decisions. Your identity as a self-sufficient adult falls to pieces. If only you could wear a sign saying, *If I were back home, I'd be a pro at this.* Leaving your comfort zone is a humble road, and because you've taken it, you have compassion for all who are uncertain, insecure, or stretched by life. You know the courage and strength it takes to talk to a stranger, start a new job, learn a new language, or admit a mistake. You can extend empathy to others, remembering how much it meant when others did the same to you.

A few years ago I walked the 790 km *Camino de Santiago* pilgrimage in Spain. I carried everything I needed for my survival and entertainment in a 34-litre backpack. I'd walk for six or seven hours, find a hostel, feed myself, sleep in a dorm full of strangers, and do it over again the next day. In the early hours one morning, I slipped down the marble staircase at the hostel. Falling is bad, and falling down a staircase is worse. I was already stretched physically, emotionally, and mentally. I didn't speak the language; I was traveling alone; I was tired and in pain. And now I was sprawled out on the bottom of the stairs, shocked and bleeding. My comfort zone was long gone.

It was the kindness of strangers that got me off the floor, to the doctor, through that day, and kept me moving along the trail. I discovered being out of my comfort zone isn't such an awful place to be. I was weak and in need of help, and a community of people carried me through—just as they did in my comfort zone. Life out of the comfort zone isn't a complete wasteland of chaos and suffering. You'll find those in and out of the comfort zone, but you'll discover there is joy and love and beauty to be found wherever you are. Take courage.

THIRTEEN

The Gift of Responsibility

 "I wish the ring had never come to me. I wish none of this had happened."

"So do all who live to see such times, but that is not for them to decide. All we have to decide is what to do with the time that is given to us."

—Frodo and Gandalf, from the film "The Fellowship of the Ring"

Do you remember the first time you were trusted with an important responsibility? There was almost a physical weight to what was asked of you. The pride you felt at being trusted was as strong as the fear of making a mistake. The message of responsibility is that you're capable and dependable. It says you've got something to contribute, and your efforts matter. You're not a spectator watching from a distance; you have skin in the game, and you have power to shape what happens. It feels amazing to be respected and trusted, but it's terrifying, too. What if you don't have the knowledge or skill or courage after all? What if you fail, let people down, and lose their respect? Maybe it's better to avoid responsibility so your weakness is never revealed.

But responsibilities don't always knock before they come in. Sometimes you choose them, and sometimes they're given to you. Responsibility asks a lot, but it gives a lot, too. It demands your time and attention. It requires you to learn new skills, ask for help, create plans and revise them. You must see the big picture and consider the needs of others. Responsibility comes with stress and pressure, and if there are other people involved, there will be conflict. You'll make judgment calls some people won't like. You'll question yourself; you'll want to give up; and you'll think about running away. You may resent the burden of responsibility and doubt it offers any gift at all, but as you carry responsibility, you become stronger. You learn to gather input from others, make hard decisions, and trust your judgment. You learn to predict consequences and anticipate future needs. You become familiar with the tension of reaching a goal while caring for people. Responsibility invites you to do more and be more than you are now; it calls you to grow and develop.

I first connected responsibility with character development by observing kids in a large family I knew. In that family, the children had more chores than I did growing up, and a lot more people to think about. There was always something to clean, someone to entertain, or a meal to prepare. Mom and Dad worked hard, and everyone was responsible for something; the youngest daughter took care of the cat. I was expecting a family of overworked, resentful, grumpy kids, but instead I saw kind, patient, caring children. I was impressed, and I was jealous.

I was jealous because daily life was teaching these kids some of the skills and attitudes I still needed to learn. My childhood home had required very little from me, and I spent my days thinking mostly about myself. With so little responsibility, I missed many lessons in consideration, generosity, and more. These kids had been given a gift I'd missed out on: the gift of responsibility.

Or at least, a gift I'd missed out on at first: at age ten, however, I was given a crash course in responsibility. From that time on I grew up in a single-parent home. Overnight, I became responsible for a load of extra tasks. I learned to set an alarm clock and get myself up and ready for school. I learned to do laundry, prepare meals, and put myself to bed. At the beginning it was rough, but gradually my competency and capacity grew. I learned to schedule time and manage my social and academic life. I learned to solve problems and make decisions. I entertained, motivated, and policed myself. It cost me something to learn these lessons so early, but what I gained still benefits me today.

It can be difficult to know how much responsibility to carry. Some of us take on too much, and others shy away from any at all. What's helped me is having people in my life who see the big picture of what's on my plate: work, family, finances, health, church, friendships, and so on. These trusted friends offer their perspective on what's enough and what's too much, protecting me from dangerous burdens and encouraging me to develop and grow.

Sometimes the burden of responsibility is more connected to how you carry it than what you carry. When I walked across Spain, I started off with a poorly adjusted backpack. Some straps were too long; others were too loose; my gear was out of balance, and my pack rubbed in awful places. Thankfully, a fellow pilgrim noticed my discomfort and suggested changes. Thank God for shifts and modifications!

Not every difficult responsibility gets easier with the tightening of a strap, but there's much to be said for learning from the experience of others. Some of what you carry will be with you for life, so don't be surprised if it takes a while to get your system sorted out. Seeing responsibility as a gift that adds value to your life can make it easier for you to bear its weight with grace and courage.

There's no doubt responsibility asks something from you. Everything's hard when you don't know how to do it. It's okay to ask for help. Be patient with yourself when you're learning the ropes. Remind yourself of difficult and scary things you've learned to do well (lead meetings, speak in public, cook rice). When you say yes to appropriate responsibility, it offers you two gifts—what you gain through carrying these weights; and the skill, presence, and service you're able to offer others. If you can receive responsibility as a gift, it will train you and grow you. Take it seriously, and give it the best you can. You're capable of much more than you know.

FOURTEEN

The Gift of Challenging Situations

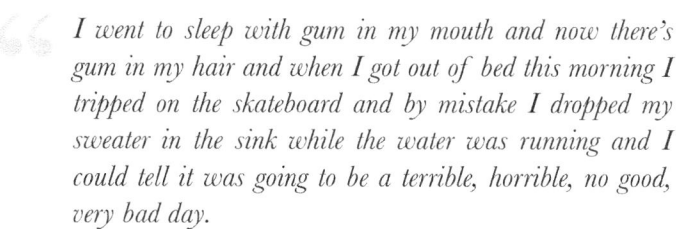
> *I went to sleep with gum in my mouth and now there's gum in my hair and when I got out of bed this morning I tripped on the skateboard and by mistake I dropped my sweater in the sink while the water was running and I could tell it was going to be a terrible, horrible, no good, very bad day.*
>
> —Judith Viorst, *Alexander and the Terrible, Horrible, No-Good, Very Bad Day*

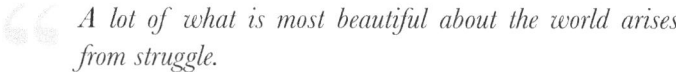
> *A lot of what is most beautiful about the world arises from struggle.*
>
> —Malcolm Gladwell, *Reader's Digest* interview

Next time you feel the familiar twinge—*This is harder than I thought it was going to be*—realize you've been given a gift. A challenging situation isn't automatically bad, but it usually comes with moments of discomfort or tension. It's challenging and stressful to land your dream job, move to a new city, have a baby, or get married, just as it's challenging and stressful to deal with a death, illness, or other loss. Challenges come from many directions, and admitting something's difficult doesn't make you a wimp or mean you want to change your mind or give up. All it means is you're being pressed and stretched, and there's no shame in that.

Not many people enjoy exams, but when you know a test's coming you study your notes and push yourself to clarify the hazy areas. If you don't know the scope of the test, it's hard to study; but when the expectations are clear, you can prepare. After the test you review your results to see what you did right and wrong. Measuring successes and failures shows you where you stand and helps you move forward.

Challenging situations are life's unofficial tests. They reflect the true state of things and provide genuine feedback on your capabilities, your weaknesses, and the resources you've stored up for emergencies. It's hard to know how you'll react when things get hard, but when the phone call comes, the test begins. Unplanned situations and crises are a wake-up call of sorts, and you may find you're not as prepared or strong or capable as you thought. But you're likely to discover strength and resilience you didn't expect. You keep going even when things are tough. You don't crumple like a scarecrow or burst like a soap bubble. You have compassion, courage, and determination to offer. Yes, there are meltdowns and freak outs, but those hard moments unearth your strength and faith and kindness.

Challenging situations allow for self-examination. In hindsight, you review and then prepare for next time. What was it like to deal with that challenge? What did you notice about yourself and your responses? What helped you manage the fear and stress? How did you treat your loved ones? How long did it take you to turn to God or ask for help? How sturdy were your support structures and relationships?

Challenges and hard things can purify us, burn away what doesn't matter, and bring wisdom. When you meet people with clear priorities and a deep sense of what matters to them, chances are you've met people who've experienced hardship. Larry Crabb writes, "No one loves well who hasn't suffered."[1] In the face of loss or tragedy or suffering, we hold on to the people who matter and let everything else drop away. There's no room for what we used to worry about—what people think, how we look, what car we drive. Like a window framing our view, hard things limit what we see.

Challenging situations grow our capacity to care and empathize. When things are rough, we're forced to accept help from others. We can't make it on our own, and we learn to accept and receive. It's a humbling but beautiful experience. Then, as time goes on, we become the ones who are able to offer this comfort to others.[2] In this way, our suffering and pain doesn't go to waste. What we have endured trains us to connect with others in their pain, and we have learned to listen with compassion.

As a child of divorce, it's rewarding for me to talk with others who grew up in broken homes. Shared loss and pain bring people together in a unique way. Listening to those with similar pains to mine has brought me great joy. Being able to say, "I understand some of what you describe, because my parents are divorced, too," allows me to participate in another's healing. In this way the most painful experience of my life has resulted in a gift I'm able to give to others. Perhaps the same is true for many of us—the awful and heartbreaking things can be transformed into a gift. Challenging situations shape us. They etch lessons and values and people in our minds and hearts, and if we're lucky, we have quality people by our side when things are hard. These people and what we go through together make our lives rich and significant and beautiful.

There is much we can do today to strengthen ourselves for the unscheduled tests of life. Remembering where we've come from and how past challenges have brought us to today is a great place to start. Making a habit of noticing God's care and presence in the easy, normal days helps us look to Him when things are hard. All the difficult stuff we've been through in the past isn't wasted when those experiences shape us into people who have strength, care, calm, and hope to extend to others.

FIFTEEN

The Gift of Going For A Walk

The best remedy for those who are afraid, lonely or unhappy is to go outside, somewhere where they can be quite alone with the heavens, nature and God.
   —Anne Frank, *The Diary of a Young Girl*

If we had a keen vision and feeling of all ordinary life, it would be like hearing the grass grow and the squirrel's heart beat, and we should die of that roar which lies on the other side of silence. As it is, the quickest of us walk about well-wadded with stupidity.
   —George Eliot, *Middlemarch*

T aking a walk is one of life's simple but overlooked gifts. Don't think of marathon training or power walking; instead, think of the kind of stroll where your feet take you wherever they please. That kind of walk invites you to be present right now and to pay attention to what's in front of you.

   To go for a walk, you must step outside the door of your

office, living room, hospital, or school and declare the realm you're leaving can survive without you, at least for a short time. You're no longer the parent, the teacher, the boss, the worker, or the glue that holds everything together. You're an earth-bound pedestrian, putting one foot in front of the other. When you go for a wander, you're just *you*—no title or responsibility or clipboard. There's nothing you must accomplish, and there's no agenda. You have time, space, motion, rhythm, and a body working in sync to move you forward.

It's easy to rush though life, getting from here to there as fast as possible. We walk through parks we don't enjoy, drive past scenery we don't notice, and look left and right at intersections and see nothing but the cars coming our direction. If we're not careful, we become blind to what surrounds us. So, as you step into the world, do your best to pay attention. In every direction there are things to see, hear, smell, and touch. When's the last time you really saw the colours, felt the textures, or enjoyed the breeze? Look up at the leaves and branches dancing in the wind. Bend down to touch the earth. What do you hear when you close your eyes? How does the air smell? What does your skin tell you about the day? Pay attention to your body as you walk. Can you feel its strength and energy? Where does it ache and protest? This is the only body you'll get, so keep an eye on what shape it's in, and remember you're the one who's supposed to care for it.

Going for a walk reminds you that you're strong and powerful, yet simultaneously tiny and weak. You occupy a small place in a very large world. In an instant one of the trees or buildings or trucks nearby could crush you. Yet this does not frighten you. You are small, but capable. You've learned to navigate this world of gravity and crosswalks. You're a natural at piloting yourself, and your track record is impressive. It takes no special equipment to go for a walk. All you need has been given to you. As you move through the streets, you explore your world and exercise your autonomy. Unlike the huge trees and impressive landmarks that surround you, you can move and change. You have a say in what your life will be.

Going for a walk reminds you that the world is vibrant and in motion. It operates without your assistance. It follows its own rules, never pausing to ask for advice or permission. As you walk, you're reminded it's a gift to exist in this world. Gravity draws you to the earth, and physics lets you push off from it with each step. You breathe in deeply, lungs expanding, then let the air out slowly. You consider the kindness of each tree quietly changing carbon dioxide to oxygen for your benefit. You are part of something bigger, receiving from those who have gone before, determined to contribute to those who are to come.

Going for a walk allows you to open yourself to fresh air and perspective. It reminds you of the wonder of being small and free, able to move, part of something grand, only responsible for a very small piece of the world. Going for a walk gives you hope; surely in such a big place there are solutions to your troubles, people to love, sources of joy and strength. Going for a walk reminds you that while you're limited, you have a measure of power. It reminds you the world is a beautiful place, for even while soaked by rain or blown by wind, you can hear birdsong or watch a butterfly or see a flower growing out of the cracked concrete.

We all have times of anxiety, worry, boredom, or sorrow. We all have days we're tired of waiting, days we feel alone and overwhelmed, or days we feel stuck. These are exactly the kinds of days when going for a walk can bring the perspective we need. A walk doesn't have to be grueling or long for it to be of benefit. Open the door, give it a go, and discover what this humble gift could offer you today.

SIXTEEN

The Gift of Taking Up A Hobby

> *This is my invariable advice to people: Learn how to cook —try new recipes, learn from your mistakes, be fearless and above all have fun!*
> —Julia Child

> *You can become a joyful person... But joyfulness is a learned skill. You must take responsibility for your joy. Not your friend, not your parent, not your spouse, not your kids, not your boss—your joy is your responsibility.*
> —John Ortberg, *The Life You've Always Wanted*

Do you have a hobby? Something you do for fun—an activity that rewards you with joy, delight, renewed energy, and perspective? If not, now's a great time to pick one and get into it. The particular hobby you choose doesn't matter much. The gift of a hobby is space and permission to learn and discover. Normal life expects you to be capable and confident, but hobbies let you put all that aside.

Hobbies are meant to be refreshing, but I'll warn you, they

come with moments of confusion, frustration, and discomfort. In the world of hobby, you're not an expert. You're interested and curious, but you don't have it all figured out. It may take time to adjust your expectations of yourself and step into the role of a beginner. Consider this: in my "day job" as a teacher, I'm the person with experience and knowledge. I stand at the front, give instructions, and correct mistakes. In my hobby world, however, I pay someone to give the instructions and point out my mistakes (not my favourite bit, but necessary). In the world of hobby, I'm free to experiment and give it a go. In that place I have permission to look and sound goofy; I invite someone to lead me and correct me and introduce me to unknown steps and sounds. Learning *Brazilian Capoeira* or Balboa dancing gives me the chance to stretch my brain, develop uniquely random skills, branch out from what's familiar, and laugh at myself.

Including hobbies in my life keeps me curious and teachable, builds my ability to focus, and reminds me of the value of perseverance. Having something in my life I'm not good at (yet) gives me compassion and empathy for my students and for people in general. Without continually learning new things, I forget how it feels to be confused, overwhelmed, and intimidated.

Taking up a hobby makes your world bigger. It might not advance your career or get you a raise, but a hobby can reduce fear, shrink insecurity, build confidence, cultivate problem-solving, and reward you with practical skills. Hobbies bring new relationships and experiences. They provide outlets for your curiosity and allow you to approach the world in a different role and with a different set of expectations and responsibilities. There's more to you than what you produce or how much you earn. A hobby lets you be a novice or a geek, and it removes the pressure to be an expert. The number of things you're terrible at will always outnumber what you're good at, and there's no shame in this. You have permission to be a beginner, make mistakes, and ask for help.

So why not study a language or learn to make croissants? Maybe now's the time to take up crocheting, the clarinet, or hairdressing. Dust off your old skateboard or snowboard. Learn to tie a hundred different knots, ice climb, or make clothes. Fold origami or join a quartet (research which instruments are in a quartet first). Take a class in massage therapy or figure skating or organic cooking. Think about how much cooler you'd be if you could tap dance or play the accordion or write poetry. If you want to be an interesting person, find something to be interested in.[1] What you learn and discover will open your eyes to a whole new world, which is a wonderful gift to give yourself, and if you stick with your hobby, it won't be long before you'll have something amazing to offer others.

SEVENTEEN

The Gift of Being Present

Love and hurry are fundamentally incompatible. Love always takes time, and time is one thing hurried people don't have.
      —John Ortberg, *The Life You've Always Wanted*

If only you could sense how important you are to the lives of those you meet; how important you can be to people you may never even dream of. There is something of yourself that you leave at every meeting with another person.
      —Fred Rogers, Mister Rogers' Neighborhood: "Thoughts for All Ages"

I lived in Asia for a number of years, and a saying I learned early on is, "Never visit someone empty-handed." In a culture that values hospitality, a considerate guest always brings a gift. It doesn't have to be extravagant or expensive, but your hands mustn't be empty when you arrive at the front door. We don't have a saying like that in Canada, but being able to contribute and give to others is one of our cultural values as well.

Choosing the right gift can be stressful. Visit a shopping mall before Christmas and you'll find frenzied shoppers searching for the perfect gift. I've bought plenty of poorly chosen gifts in a moment of panic, and I've received a fair share of similar gifts too. And while I'm grateful for the sentiment behind every gift, I've often thought it would be nicer to receive my friend's time and the chance to connect rather than another item. The gift of presence is of great value, but many of us overlook the gift of ourselves, never considering what a treasure it would be to offer our time and attention to others.

Mother Teresa, an incredible woman who dedicated her life to caring for the poorest of the poor, observed, "The most terrible poverty is loneliness, and the feeling of being unloved." Humans are made for connection and closeness. We all long to be valued, appreciated, known, heard, and seen. We need to know we matter and to believe our life is important to others.

So the question is, how do we show the people we love that they are valuable to us? One of the best ways is by being present. Being present has to do with making space for the person you're with, giving your attention and focus to them, and using self-discipline to resist distractions. When you're present, you offer yourself as a listener; you empathize, laugh, cry, or celebrate. You're active and engaged, letting the other person know they matter, they are significant, and they are your priority.

Being present means you stay in the moment, whether alone or with someone else. When you're present, you notice and absorb elements of your surroundings. Rather than thinking about what will happen tomorrow morning or analyzing a conversation from yesterday, you pay attention to what you experience now; you savour the joy or happiness or satisfaction of this moment. Being present is similar to living in slow motion. There's time to notice the angle of the sun, the softness or scratchiness of your sweater, the background music, or the cool breeze. Being present and attentive are ways we embrace and enjoy the peace, hope, and friendship in our lives, rather than letting them pass unnoticed, floating away like a released balloon.

The opposite of being present is being busy and distracted. When we're in a constant rush, thinking about what's next, it's impossible to be where we are. Technology allows us to spend our days somewhere other than where we actually are. We may be on the bus to work but absorbed in another place. Any time of day or night, we can be in our favorite TV show or at the wedding of a friend from high school. We could be on vacation in Hawaii or skiing in Switzerland. Then, when we get to where we're headed—the movies, a date, vacation, or visiting family—we're still tied to our phones, trying to be in two places at once. What's up with that? Why do we hide in our music and screens? What are we hoping to find there?

I think we've forgotten how to be *here*. We've forgotten how to concentrate, to focus, to wait, and to rest. We're in a hurry to see and experience the next thing, and we miss out on the chance to connect with the real people who are with us. Can we open our eyes to see what and who is in front of us now? What we have at the moment, what we feel and experience and see, probably isn't perfect; but it's ours, for the time being. Teaching yourself to appreciate what you have now is the only way to enjoy your actual life.[1]

Being present is a gift you can offer to others, for when you're present, you're available. You have the capacity to connect, listen, and hold space. When your mind and attention are elsewhere, people feel it; but to show up fully is an irreplaceable gift.

One way I've practiced offering my presence to others is through dance. I adore swing dancing, and it requires two people. For the three or four minutes of a song, you dance with one person, then switch to a different partner. Over the evening you dance with people of every level of skill and experience. Some dances flow while others are awkward, but to dance with your partner you must stay present and engaged. You can't check out, because the dance is dynamic and improvised. You have to hear the music, look at your partner, and watch for signals of what's coming next. You have to block out the last song and the dancers next to you. Your world shrinks to you, your partner, the floor underneath, and the beat of the music. It's tempting to get distracted and go through the motions, but to do so is to forfeit the *with* and *together* that make dancing so wonderful.

A practical way to be present to another is through listening. Active listening is a way to deepen the quality of your friendships and show love and care for others. "The feeling of not being understood is one of the most painful in human experience... When we're with someone who doesn't listen, we shut down. When we're with someone who's interested and responsive—a good listener—we perk up and come alive."[2] You could say we listen all day long, but it's possible to listen without really listening. There are ways of listening that brush people off and push them away, and it's possible to listen in ways that provide space to open up and connect. The way we sit or stand while listening communicates something to the speaker. Do I lean in and make eye contact, mirroring the sadness or excitement I see in her face, or do I stand with folded arms, glancing around the room or checking my watch? Do I have a habit of interrupting people when they speak, either from excitement or impatience, or do I leave space for them to elaborate, asking for more details to let them know I'm interested in what they've experienced and are thinking about?

So for today, take a deep breath and look around at where you are. Lean toward people and open your eyes wider to your surroundings. Wherever you are right now is the life you've been given for today. Do your best to be present, seeing today as God's gift to you, knowing you yourself are a gift you can share with others.

EIGHTEEN

The Gift of Gratitude

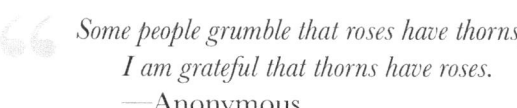

Some people grumble that roses have thorns;
I am grateful that thorns have roses.
—Anonymous

How my eyes see, perspective, is my key to enter into His
gates. I can only do so with thanksgiving. If my inner eye
has God seeping up through all things, then can't I give
thanks for anything?
—Ann Voskamp, *One Thousand Gifts*

Like many of us, I have a bad habit of focusing on the negative and skimming over what's good. Studies show we're more likely to remember criticism than affirmation, and it puzzles me that we stubbornly clutch the negative and quickly release the good. For some reason the mean comments and harsh judgments stick like glue, and it's a real effort to keep what's good front and centre.

One practice that has helped me with this is gratitude. Simply defined as *the quality of being thankful,* gratitude is a willingness to approach the world with an attitude of appreciation rather than displeasure, annoyance, or bitterness. Gratitude powerfully changes the tone and atmosphere of a conversation or gathering. The benefits of gratitude include stronger social connections, better sleep, decreased anxiety, and increased joy. Who knew gratitude could offer so much?

For years I misunderstood where gratitude came from. I thought it would appear when circumstances were ideal and there was no longer any need for change or growth. I thought gratitude indicated a life of ease and abundance—qualities that didn't describe mine. I was waiting for a big break before I expressed gratitude to the people who'd helped me achieve my goals. What I didn't realize is that gratitude doesn't fall on me; it's something I can choose. Gratitude decides to recognize and be thankful for what's good and positive and beautiful, no matter what else is in the picture. Happiness is a feeling, but gratitude is an action. Gratitude doesn't require an ideal situation before it springs up. I can be unhappy and grateful at the same time. I can be lonely and grateful, angry and grateful, discouraged and grateful—you name it.

Gratitude doesn't deny what's awful or painful or wasted. It doesn't ask you to paint life with a false positivity. Gratitude doesn't tell you to give up, shut down, or accept an unacceptable situation. But because gratitude can find good even in the midst of what's awful, it provides a way to live in the tension of a world that is both wonderful and heart-breaking. You can express gratitude even while you seek change, or feel frustrated, or work to achieve unmet goals. You don't have to wait for success or utopia before you say *thanks*. Cynicism paints life with a dark brush, refusing to acknowledge any hint of beauty or goodness, but gratitude notices sparkles in the rubble and streaks of colour in the clouds.

Gratitude draws your attention to what you have even as

you note what's missing or broken. Gratitude refuses to let what's bad or wrong have the final word. In that way, gratitude requires very little at all. Like a delighted grandmother who remarks, "How lovely, my dear!" no matter what you say or do, gratitude doesn't demand perfection before it speaks. Gratitude, like kindness and hope, can show up anywhere, at any time. Gratitude is a place of refuge and comfort you can turn to in frustration, disappointment, loneliness, or fear. There's freedom in saying, "I choose to be grateful for today and the good I see, even if there's work to be done and much I didn't choose."

If you're not sure how to build your gratitude muscles, you can begin by looking at your childhood. Think of those who helped you before you asked. Make a gratitude list for the doctor who delivered you, the nurse who held you, or the teachers who helped you learn to read and write and do math —even the bus drivers who got you to school, and the janitors who ensured it was kept clean. You may not remember their names, but without them you wouldn't be where you are. Next, move on to your youth. What would you say to the coaches who inspired you to grow, the musicians who wrote your favourite songs, or the boss who gave you your first job? What about the friends and family who laughed at your jokes and loved you though your bad moods? Your list could get very, very long—for you have been given a lot.

Eventually you'll get to today. Today may be a great or a horrible day, but you can start wherever you are. At times I walk through my house and look at what fills it. I'm grateful for the farmers who grow the coffee I drink, for the workers who take away my garbage. I remember meals around my table, or the friend I was with when I bought my butter dish. I look at cookies my neighbour dropped off, the quilt my grandma made. I'm grateful for the mailman who carries letters to my door each day, for the friend who sends a card, and for my job that pays the bills. As I remember what I've been given, I practice saying *thank you*. Expressing gratitude changes something in me, and it changes the people I thank. When I express gratitude to *someone* for *something*, I shatter the lie that I'm on my own and no one cares for me. I have been given so much; I have benefitted from the beauty others offer to the world.

I don't need everything on my wish list before I exercise gratitude. I can express gratitude today for the *enough* I have right now; I don't have to wait for something more. Gratitude adds value to every cup of coffee, every sunny day, my favourite song, a comfortable bed, a meal with friends, or a clean pair of socks. Noticing these things, instead of letting them pass by, reminds me I'm blessed—I'm rich—and I've been given more than I realize.[1] Gratitude is free to anyone who wants to learn it, and as we grow in gratitude, it changes us into people who carry hope and kindness with us into every situation.

NINETEEN

The Gift of Waiting

We are uncomfortable with stillness, waiting, being, contemplation, yielding, receiving, with ambiguity, the intangible, the hidden, the secret, the absorbing… We see waiting as wasting.
—Gertrud Mueller Nelson, *Here All Dwell Free*

Rest is the ultimate humiliation because in order to rest, we must admit we are not necessary, that the world can get along without us, that God's work does not depend on us.
—Michael Yaconelli, *Messy Spirituality*

Years ago a friend told me about her "twenty-four hour shopping rule." Before making any unplanned purchase over fifty dollars, she would wait twenty-four hours. This rule saved her a ton of money and kept her from accumulating a house full of junk, because often enough her desire for that thing had faded by the next day. The

twenty-four hour rule opened my eyes to the benefits of waiting. Maybe you're okay with waiting; maybe it drives you nuts;
but no matter how well you plan, there are times you have to
wait. And really, it's not all bad. You wait for flowers to bloom,
kittens to be born, Christmas morning, the first snowfall, or
the rain clouds to go away. You wait for calls that never come,
lost packages, or jobs that are offered to other people. Life
takes time, and we're used to that; but where are the gifts
offered to us in it?

First of all, when you wait for something, your world gets
smaller; and the smaller your world, the more you can pay
attention to what it contains. Whether you're waiting for a bus
or waiting for a baby, you put other things aside and keep your
eyes on your hope. You say *no* to the other places you could go
and things you could do, and you stay focused. You wait with
expectation, even if the evidence isn't visible.

Waiting also makes your world bigger. Waiting creates a
gap between now and when the waiting comes to an end. In
that gap, you have time to imagine other possibilities and
opportunities. You can daydream and brainstorm; you can
look up and around; you can imagine a different ending than
the one you have in mind. While the power's out or the oil's
being changed or the pie's baking in the oven, you can pause
and think and rest. Often we fill these moments with something else, never giving ourselves permission to breathe and
reflect, but what's the harm in using the moments waiting
brings to think about what *could* be?

Not everything you wait for is guaranteed to happen.
There are times that waiting feels like a pointless, miserable
waste of time. Waiting with uncertainty forces you to look at
your fears and hopes and motives. Will the promotion you're
waiting for prove you're good enough? Will your efforts at
reconciliation finally lead to peace and harmony? Will the

spouse or child you long for provide the happiness you desire? Are you holding on to something because you're afraid to let go, or because it's too important to forget? There are many reasons to wait, and they all come with a cost. Waiting tests and purifies you, checks to see how determined and committed you are. How long you'll wait reveals how important something is. It's okay to let time and space put things into perspective for you, just like the twenty-four hour rule does for my friend.

Waiting reminds us of our limitations. We can't control the whole world, and we don't always get our way. Not everything we want comes with a *click here* button and one-day delivery. Surrendering the need to force and control is easier said than done. And while the idea of speeding up time or slowing it down sounds appealing, it's a good thing we can't. The slow, steady march of time brings stability to our world, and we need stability. The hard and boring parts of waiting teach us patience and perseverance, and slowing down allows us to savour the wonderful things when they come. There's something freeing and comforting in trusting the process, and think of all we'd miss if everything happened instantly.

So let's do our best to enjoy the times of waiting when they come. Let's embrace the process, take the time to look at what we have, and to remember—we need a lot less than we think.

TWENTY

The Gift of Belonging

One of the most important aspects to growth in our suffering is that we need to know that we are understood. This is what empathy provides for us. We cannot grow if we are all alone emotionally. Life is too difficult.
—Henry Cloud and John Townsend, *How People Grow*

I belong to the people I love, and they belong to me—they, and the love and loyalty I give them, form my identity far more than any word or group ever could.
—Veronica Roth, *Allegiant*

The search for belonging and connection is part of the human experience. Friends and strangers have confessed to me, "I'm not sure where I belong," and I've wondered the same myself. Many of us struggle to find our people and a place of connection. We've been on the outside, looking in, wondering how to cross from one side to the other.

What are we looking for when we speak of belonging? Like the idea of *home*, it can be difficult to articulate. We want to be known and appreciated. We want security and people to depend on. We want adventures and celebrations to look forward to. We want rides to the airport and help moving boxes. We want a safe place where we can let down our guard and come as we are.

This longing for connection, even when unmet, indicates something positive. The desire to belong is a factory-setting for humans. We're built to need others, to give and receive, and to be part of something. But we're told autonomy and independence are marks of success, so we learn to conceal our needs and struggle to make sense of these conflicting messages. We work hard to "do it on our own," push away the help that's offered, and hold back what we could give others, even as we long for the support and connection of belonging.

I've come to discover that belonging is an entity on the move. When you want to merge onto the highway, you have to keep moving. If you slam on the brakes, you'll never enter the flow; and once you're at a complete stop, it's almost impossible to join the traffic. Finding belonging is similar. Belonging's an active state, not passive; so keep moving forward. To merge with a community, you have to offer a bit of yourself, expose some weakness, and be known for who you are. There's no guarantee it will be one hundred percent safe, and this can be terrifying. It makes sense to hesitate before offering ourselves to others, but until we take those first steps, disconnection and loneliness will follow us. As Brené Brown says, "In the absence of love and belonging, there is always suffering." If we don't find places of safety and connection, there will be suffering. We stay on guard, protecting ourselves, striving and performing, and it's exhausting.

But things don't have to stay as they are. Community and

belonging can be built; not by yourself, and not overnight, but it's possible. Community might not look the way you imagine, for it comes in many shapes and is built from unlikely people. I had many ideals about community, one of which involved a modern yellow-brick road to guide me to my destination. I was waiting for a sign to tell me *this is it!* But all I found were groups of regular people doing normal things, inviting me to join along.

Part of my problem was that I had confused the sequence of events and was approaching community backward. I wanted to click with a perfect community, then offer myself to the group. But belonging grows as and while we invest in relationships, not before. Relationships have to be planted before they can grow. Commitment and participation allow connection and trust to develop.

Communities have cultures and personalities, just like families, and not all of them are created equal. Unlike family, however, you get to pick the community you're part of. It's a dance to discover where you fit, and not every partner jives with you. It's okay to be picky when you choose a community; after all, there's only so much of you to go around.

Once you identify a potential community, make it a priority to participate in what's going on. You can't grow closer to people you don't spend time with. You'll have to endure small talk, awkward silences, and repeat your life story many times, but try to be patient. You can't rush the process of getting to know people. And think about it this way—every friend you've ever had started out as a stranger.

Show up and look for ways to contribute. Can you bake muffins, make coffee, or manage a website? You have unique talents and a one-of-a-kind personality, so don't be afraid to show up as you. Bring those amazing Oreo fudge brownies or your signature seven-layer dip. Don't just drift in and drift back out. Bring something of yourself and make an effort. As you contribute to the group, your sense of ownership and connection grows. As you offer your ideas and talents to the group, there's a shift from "them" to "us."

Be willing to expand your circle of relationships. It's natural to gravitate toward people like you, but you'll miss out on what you could learn from others. Get to know someone older or younger, someone in a different season of life, someone from another country, or someone whose daily life is different from yours. You're not the only one who wants to connect and be included, so invite a new friend over for mac and cheese, meet up at the park with a thermos of hot chocolate, or throw a party to celebrate something in your life.

There's an ebb and flow to community; there are glorious moments and low points. It's likely you'll be disappointed at some point, maybe even hurt or offended; but there's a strength in community that's worth fighting for. We're all learning about loving and caring for each other, so bring what you know and who you are to the mix, and in this way everyone can benefit and learn together.

TWENTY-ONE

The Gift of Intentional Friendship

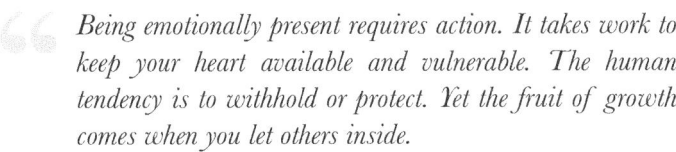

Being emotionally present requires action. It takes work to keep your heart available and vulnerable. The human tendency is to withhold or protect. Yet the fruit of growth comes when you let others inside.
    —Henry Cloud and John Townsend, *How People Grow*

Go through your phone book, call people and ask them to drive you to the airport. The ones who will drive you are your true friends. The rest aren't bad people; they're just acquaintances.
    —Jay Leno

I t takes a lot of effort to make friends when you're an adult. I was in my thirties, recently moved to a new city, before I realized how clueless I was about making friends. My experience as a kid and teenager had spoiled me. As a kid my bestie was the person in the desk next to me at school. This effortless way of finding friends left me unprepared for the adult world.

As an adult, the pool of potential friends is huge, which sounds promising… but everyone's busy with work and school and dating. You're lucky to get a person's name—let alone other clues about who would make a good friend—before they zip past. You can be surrounded by roommates and workmates and activity but not have any friends at all.

The desire to be known and share life with others is part of our design. These desires draw us out of ourselves and motivate us to do the hard work of friendship. But acknowledging the desire for connection doesn't mean we know how to achieve it. Desires don't come with GPS coordinates. Friendships sound great in theory, but the reality doesn't always match our expectations. It's possible to build your contact list while the quality of your friendships decline. While every *like* and follower gives a brief rush, these interactions don't compare with being understood or valued. Our cultural values of quick, easy, and disposable make quality friendships tough, because friendships take time; they ask a lot from you; and when you see people as disposable, you're in trouble.

As a kid it was nice to have friends handed to me on a platter. Those friendships taught me about unconditional love and getting along with almost anyone, but there's a great gift in intentional friendship. When a friendship takes effort, you're forced to decide how important it is to you. You have a say in what the friendship is like. You get to shape how you connect and encourage each other. You build a culture together, deciding how your shared values and priorities will be expressed.

Motivational speaker Jim Rohn says, "You are the average of the five people you spend the most time with," and we all know people rub off on us. The quality of our friendships impacts the quality of our life—for good and bad. When your inner circle is strong, your life's more stable. It's easier to face the challenges of the day with less fear and more hope. With secure friendships, the good things in life are better, and awful things are less bad. You can take risks and be generous. But weak and unstable relationships affect every part of your life. It's hard to grow and thrive when you feel lonely or unwanted. Every day is a struggle when unhealthy friends pull you down and suck the life out of you.

Because of the way friends influence us, it's helpful to take stock of your friendships from time to time. What strengths and weaknesses do you see in your friendships? How healthy are they? Do you feel supported, valued, and appreciated by your friends? In what ways are you supporting and caring for them? Does anything need to change?

One beautiful thing about friendships is that they don't have to stay where they are. They can go deeper; they can change; and you can let some of them go. It's normal for dating couples to *define the relationship*, so why not do the same thing with your friends? If you'd like deeper friendships, chat about what it would look like to be more committed or vulnerable. Friendships, like any other living thing, benefit from regular attention and maintenance.

While we all need friends, friendships aren't based on primarily on need, but on want. We need the dentist to pull a tooth, but we want to share our vacation with friends. There's something satisfying about being needed, but being wanted is even better. It's important to have friends who delight in us and think we're worth their time.[1] Friendship reminds us over and over again, in a hundred insignificant ways, *You are valued. You are worth an investment of time and energy. Being in your presence brings me joy*. It's a great privilege to have people who see our faults, know our story, and still want to share life with us. So let's celebrate the gift of friendship, and let's put effort and energy into making the friendships we have as healthy and honest as they can be. Friendship is a gift we give and receive, and when it's done well, friendship is its own goal and reward.

TWENTY-TWO

The Gift of Confession

… You find sometimes that a Thing which seemed very Thingish inside you is quite different when it gets out into the open and has other people looking at it.
—A. A. Milne, *The House at Pooh Corner*

If we say we have no sin, we are deceiving ourselves and the truth is not in us. If we confess our sins, He is faithful and righteous to forgive us our sins and to cleanse us from all unrighteousness.
—1 John 1:8-9 (NASB)

There are a lot of things I enjoy about sci-fi stories, but one futuristic idea I can't really get excited about is mind-reading. Could you imagine never keeping a secret or having a private life? What if your every thought and action were put on display? What if everybody knew everything you've ever said or done? Thanks, but no thanks. Boundaries and filters are beautiful things.

We all feel the tension between knowledge and privacy.

Honesty and transparency are valuable things, but you can't have healthy relationships unless you can decide what to retain and what to reveal, when to open up and when to hold back. Choosing with whom and how much to share is one of our dearest freedoms, and it's not always easy to know when to be open and when to be guarded.

One of my challenges when it comes to being open with people is figuring out how to be honest about the hard, shameful, frustrating stuff. I've tried hiding it, covering it over, and pretending it wasn't there, but that didn't work so well. Then, a few years ago, a friend and I discovered a spiritual discipline called *confession*.[1] It took a while to get the hang of it, but practicing it has changed both of us, and it's proved to be a more productive way of dealing with shame and guilt than hiding.[2]

The discipline of confession gives me a way to be honest and open with another person about the difficult (even the dark and questionable) parts of my life. Confession begins when I explore what's going on inside. Before I can be honest with my confessor, I have to be honest with myself. What am I truly thinking and feeling? What's underneath my struggle or fear or temptation? It's good to be known and to have help sorting out the mess. Confession isn't about venting or complaining. Instead it's a place to walk in humble vulnerability with another person for the sake of understanding, change, and freedom. The sooner I notice and confess, the sooner I can be free.

Confession requires self-awareness and trust. I reach out to my confessor and describe my pain or loneliness or rejection. I tell her the judgments I've made and my plans to strike back at the person who hurt me. I describe my envy or fear or apathy. Admitting my thoughts and feelings clears the fog. I begin to put the brakes on destructive plans before they come to life. My heart rate slows. I can take deep breaths. A weight lifts from my shoulders. Confession helps me interrupt myself *before* I do what I don't want to do. Confession doesn't prevent every bad decision, but it slows me down, helps me make better choices, and reminds me it's possible to say *no* to the very tempting thing I want to do.

When I tell my confessor the ugly things I've done or imagined, and she listens without flinching, I discover my fear of rejection is an illusion. My sins do not separate me from God. As I confess and repent, I find the forgiveness and welcome of the Father. His arms are open wide to me, and the kindness of my confessor reminds me I'm loved, even in my brokenness. Confession unburdens my soul. My wrongs, hurts, and sins don't define me. Angry feelings, longing for what I don't have, and dreams of revenge aren't the end of the story. Temptation draws my attention to an area in need of help, and as I confess, I receive kindness, compassion, and peace.

My confessor isn't responsible to stop or change me; I'm responsible for myself. But confession reminds me I don't have to face the hard parts of life alone. Confession is a step toward a more connected way of living. When I feel alone, stressed, or neglected, it's only a matter of time before I go down a bad path. Confession helps me reach out to another person instead of pulling back and trying to do it alone. It takes courage to trust someone with my pain and shame, but every step away from fear and toward connection is a step in a better direction.

The practice of confession gives us a picture of God's unconditional love. Confession doesn't excuse sin; it tells us we're not rejected in our struggles. God invites us to come to Him with our burdens and needs. There's an abundance of grace, of kindness, of forgiveness, and of compassion in God's heart. From our understanding of who God is, we're able to say to one another, "I care about you, and you're not alone. That situation sounds hard, and I'm here for you. With God's help, there's a way forward."

What a gift it is to have someone see our darkest parts and still welcome our friendship. What a gift it is to know we can come as we are into the presence of God and others and find the love and welcome we need. Through the practice of confession, as we make space for the hard and hidden parts of life, as we share our sin and pain with each other, we participate in God's work of healing and restoration, one confession at a time.

TWENTY-THREE

The Gift of Knowing What Story You're In

I can only answer the question "What am I to do?" if I can answer the prior question "Of what story or stories do I find myself a part?"
— Alasdair MacIntyre, *After Virtue*

A good storyteller speaks something into nothing. Where there is an absence of story, or perhaps a bad story, a good storyteller walks in and changes reality. He doesn't critique the existing story, or lament about his boredom, like a critic. He just tells something different and invites other people into the new story he is telling.
— Donald Miller, *A Million Miles in a Thousand Years*

It's not just me who likes stories; everyone loves them. I know this because the fiction section of a bookstore is always larger than the sections of cookbooks and art history. We spend a lot of time telling and retelling stories, analyzing them, laughing or crying about them, or coming up with better endings for the ones that disappoint us. Stories aren't reserved for bookstores or libraries, either. We're all in the middle of a story of our own—a story rich and colourful, full of twists and turns. From our earliest memories to what happened this afternoon, our lives are comprised of good and bad characters, plot twists, rising action, climaxes, and tension. What we've lived through and discovered along the way helps us make sense of what's going on and why it matters.

I didn't see my life this way until recently, however. Previously, I'd lived under the impression that *story* was only for famous people who had power to direct their lives. Those people had choices and purpose. Those people could make an impact, create change, bring hope, fix the world's problems, and give the rest of us something to aspire to. I was normal and regular. My role was to accept what was given to me, go through the motions, and be thankful things weren't any worse.

In past years I've come to see I have a story, too, and my story is as legit as anyone's. As humans, we're wired for story. We expect the world to have heroes and villains, quests and rewards, victims and bystanders and extras. We unconsciously place ourselves in the stories around us. It's possible to be a sidekick in one story, the hero in another, and an extra in a third. What I tell myself about my story and my role in each story is like a path through a forest. The more I walk down the path, the wider and clearer it gets. If I see myself as loved and courageous, I walk that path with increasing confidence. If I see myself as a weakling with nothing going for her, I naturally choose that path instead. The power of habit pulls me in a direction, even if it's not the direction I want to go.

Stories have incredible power to shape us, which is why the victors tend to write history books to benefit themselves and make themselves look good. The story you tell (and believe) declares what's true and what's important to you. It connects people and places, actions and outcomes. Story sheds light on motives and results, which is what makes it so important to examine where your information comes from. If you've ever been deceived or misunderstood, you know how easily a story can get twisted.

And while it can be frightening to discover details of your story, there are incredible benefits to knowing your origins. The best stories involve someone who wants something and has to fight to get it.[1] If the character faces her fears, sacrifices for others, forgives an enemy, or overcomes what seems impossible, the story is satisfying. When a person is transformed by hardships and struggles, we're inspired. When there's no risk, no problems, and no suffering, the story's bland and boring. We're eager to hear stories of danger and sacrifice, but we avoid getting entangled in such things ourselves. It's ironic— we want to be part of something cool and important; we want our lives to matter; we want a reason to get out of bed in the morning; but we default toward easy and comfortable and predictable.

So perhaps there's something to be gained from looking at the obstacles and opportunities of your life through the lens of story. Can you articulate its plot, your role, and the key players? Do you understand which direction the story's going? Are you aware of the backstory: the challenges faced by your parents, grandparents, and community? Knowing where you've come from helps you decide whether or not you want to continue with that storyline. You don't have to blindly accept the story handed to you. You have a say in the story you tell with your life.

The best story[2] I've encountered is the one with God at the centre. He exists as the creator and source of life. From a foundation of love and generosity, He made a place for us in the world.[3] He is the anchor of reality.[4] Because we're included in His story, we can walk through life with purpose. We can have courage and hope. In the same way an airport map tells us "You are here," we make sense of our life when we locate ourselves in God's story.

As we learn of God's character and experience His goodness, strength, and mercy at work in the world, we become more secure and free. As we receive His love, we're able to offer love to others. Being part of God's story helps us face obstacles with courage and perseverance. We no longer have to prove our significance or strive to make a name for ourselves. We're part of something bigger—a story with historical and global significance—and our contribution matters. Because the story is full of beauty and belonging, invitation, generosity, and connection, we have a reason to offer the best of ourselves to it. We're motivated to develop in character. We want to participate in the work of restoration and renewal.

Other stories are out there, too, urging us to make ourselves top priority. Some stories tell us performance and competition are the path to significance, and everyone is a competitor or critic or judge. If we see ourselves in this story, we feel alone and hopeless. Friendly faces are temporary; places of rest and belonging are illusion. Discovering and holding on to the true story of life is a battle. It takes effort to remember we were created *on* purpose and *for* a purpose. It takes energy to remember where meaning and value originate.

To navigate forward, we need the wisdom of those who have gone before. Their stories remind us we're part of something bigger; there is more going on than what's in front of us today. We need each other. None of us see everything clearly, so we must stay humble and teachable, even toward those who are different from us.

It takes courage to live in a story that's bigger than us and beyond our control. When we know our story, we can stand tall, free from shame and fear, content to do our part and trust God with the rest. There will be struggles, but struggles are part of every good story. We're transformed as we walk with God in His story, and this is a gift offered to us and a gift for us to offer others. When we see our purpose and story clearly— when it really sinks in—we're able to live in the truth that we matter, we belong, and what we do is significant.

TWENTY-FOUR

The Gift of Reflecting on God's Image

Your true identity is as a child of God. This is the identity you have to accept. Once you have claimed it and settled in it, you can live in a world that gives you much joy as well as pain...You belong to God, and it is as a child of God that you are sent into the world.
—Henri Nouwen, *The Inner Voice of Love*

Stand up and discover how beautiful you are. You have a message, a gift to give the world. We are all messengers [of Jesus], empowered to bring peace to our world and to discover that, through love and wisdom, we can build communities of love, signs of peace for our world.
—Jean Vanier, *We Need One Another*

Every once in a while you come across someone who wows you with her courage, intelligence, determination, and passion for the rights of others. Strong, articulate women like Malala Yousafzai[1], campaigning for the education of girls; Emma Watson, UN Women Goodwill

Ambassador, advocating for gender equality; or Lady Diana's work with leprosy victims and HIV patients—all are amazing examples to the rest of us. These women have used their connections, circumstances, and accomplishments to raise global awareness about important issues. It's easy to be impressed by women like these but see no way to be like them. When will I ever walk a red carpet, meet heads of state, or speak on television? Does what I say and do make a difference to anyone?

Certainly these women have a level of power and influence that's rare. When you're an ambassador or spokesperson, you're given opportunities most of us don't have. You're entrusted with a specific mandate and the reputation of those you represent. What you say, who you know, and every choice you make is watched and scrutinized. Every word is critiqued; every photo is reviewed; each sentence is analyzed for hidden meaning. Nothing is overlooked. Truly, as a representative, no part of your life is beyond notice, and it's perhaps in the *ordinary* things—your meals, your shopping, your family life— where skeptics and fans judge the integrity of your message.

I'm not an ambassador or a member of a royal family, but as a follower of Christ I've been asked to represent God to the world. If you follow Christ, this is your calling, too. God has created us to be like Him and reflect Him. As humans we're free to love, free to choose, able to relate, and able to act and respond. We can create; we have strength; we can influence; we can give and connect and dream and rejoice. As we love and follow Christ, our words, choices, habits, and loves are to be more and more congruent with His. Our lives are a living sermon communicating what He's like. What God cares about ought to be reflected in what we care about. God made us to be His image-bearers so people could look at us and get clues about what God is like.[2]

As we continue to learn what's important to God and as we experience His love, we're better able to reflect Him to those around us. As image-bearers, we bring His presence with us. We display something of what He's like, and every aspect of life is an opportunity to show the world how much God cares for them. The way we spend our time and money, how we treat strangers and foreigners, how we post on social media, and how we respond to problems and challenges carry a message. Every part of our life is important; everything we do has potential to reflect God to the world.

Being an image-bearer comes with a massive responsibility. The weight of this responsibility can freak me out—after all, there's so much I don't know, so many complicated issues, and so many situations beyond my control. But God's the one who asked us to represent Him, and He thinks we've got what it takes. He wants to teach us how to love, how to serve, how to listen, and how to live like Christ. Yes, we'll make some mistakes. Yes, we've lots to learn, but God cares about people. For all of history He's worked through and with people. He's not overwhelmed by the pain and suffering of the world; He doesn't avoid it or ignore it; He's rolled up His sleeves and stepped into the mess—through Jesus and through us. As His representatives, this is our challenge: Live in such a way that people are drawn to and curious about the One we represent. Live the kind of lives where people will look and say, "I've always wondered if people could live with such hope and joy and connection, and now I know it is possible." Don't give up. Don't lose heart; Father, Son, and Spirit promise to guide us and help us live as worthy representatives. Let's press on to know and follow Him for the joy it brings us, and for the sake of those who need to see what He's like. [3]

TWENTY-FIVE

The Gift of Growing vs. Making

The kingdom of God is like a man who casts seed upon the soil; and he goes to bed at night and gets up by day, and the seed sprouts and grows—how, he himself does not know.
—Mark 4:26-27 (NASB)

We move forward in ways that we do not even understand and through the quiet workings of time and grace. When we get there, we are never sure just how it happened, and God does not seem to care who gets the credit, as long as our growth continues.
—Richard Rohr, *Falling Upward*

When I was growing up we had a lot of houseplants, which I mostly ignored: not a lot of excitement connected to slow-moving green things. However, as an adult, I now find myself drawn to and intrigued by the presence of these living, growing life forms. I like the beauty and surprise of a plant. Out of stillness and quietness, leaves sprout and unfold; flowers may appear. A plant doesn't announce itself with noise or activity, but it reaches for the sun, cleans my air, and adds colour to my space. The gentle, gradual changes, even when agonizingly slow, offer a message I need to hear: growth is not dependent on me.

There's a wonder and mystery to living things. Unlike friends or siblings or pets, the plants gathered in my living room don't respond to my suggestions or requests. They share my space, yet they move to the beat of their own drum. They take cues from a source I can't hear, responding to rules I can't decode. Without teachers or lessons, they know when to rest, when to bloom, when to grow or shed leaves, and when to send their roots deeper. I supply the water and at times move them to adjust for sunlight, but most of what they need is other than what I provide.

Parker Palmer reflects on the difference between *making* and *growing* in his book *Let Your Life Speak*. When we view our participation in the world in terms of what we *make*, we live with a heavy burden. If our successes in career, family, business, friendships, and love are what we *make* happen, we operate from control, manipulation, and competition. We reduce everyone and everything to parts, then do what we can to arrange those parts to suit our needs and desires.

But if we see the world and its inhabitants as alive and growing, we must relate in a different way. All of life cannot be predicted and controlled. There are times of rest and waiting. Growth happens on its own schedule and takes its cues from something beyond us. The gift of growing encourages us to notice what's around us and to pay attention to the thoughts and desires of our heart. We pay attention, not to control, but to enjoy—to anticipate what's to come, and to appreciate the unique beauty of each living thing. Life's less stressful when we don't have to *make* it all happen. Just as we can't order a plant to grow, threatening it with deadlines or coaxing it with incentives, the living, dynamic entities around us are not ours to control.

Growth can be frightening because growing things change. People are unpredictable. Life is fragile. Vulnerability and risk are part of the package. Some, if not all, of our dreams are beyond what we can *make* happen, and our most precious hopes usually involve other people. We can imagine and plan and invite and prepare, but the world doesn't respond to the push and pull of buttons and levers like a machine. Our world is full of people making their own plans and dreaming their own dreams. We don't always get what we want, but if we embrace the perspective of growth, surrendering our hopes and plans to the wisdom of a God-created world where things *grow*, we can discover a joy and a peace therein.

I recently added two houseplants to my collection, and the shopkeeper warned me not to overwater them. Too much water kills houseplants more often than too little water does. Apparently plants are less thirsty than we think. His warning encouraged me to reflect on how I relate to the living things around me. Trying to give or help or fix before discerning what's needed may actually hinder growth. The urge to overwater reminds me it's difficult to let go of control. The urge to *make* our dreams come true and *make* the life we want is woven into our cultural narrative. Slowing, surrendering, and trusting God for *growth* feels uncomfortable. But until we slow down and make space for growth, it's difficult for God and others to participate in what we long for. We can't *make* healthy friendships or a strong community or a loving family by our efforts alone. These things take time; they require tending and watering and rest. When we embrace *growing*, we shrug off the pressure to *make* everything we want to happen, happen.

It takes courage and faith to live in this alive and growing world. It's hard to know when to water and when not to water. Sometimes watering in the best thing, but sometimes there's really nothing you can do to make things different than they are. Sometimes all you can do is wait and rest and trust that something will grow when the time is right. We're not alone, and it doesn't all depend on us. We're part of something big and beautiful that's designed to bring life. Below the surface, in deep places our eyes can't see, beautiful things are growing. We live in a world animated by the breath of God, and my plants whisper this to me every day.

TWENTY-SIX

The Gift of Sabbath

*I want to convince you, in part, that setting apart an
entire day, one out of seven, for feasting and resting and
worship and play is a gift and not a burden, and
neglecting the gift too long will make your soul, like soil
never left fallow, hard and dry and spent.*
    —Mark Buchanan, *The Rest of God*

*Sabbath observance invites us to stop. It invites us to rest.
It asks us to notice that while we rest, the world continues
without our help. It invites us to delight in the world's
beauty and abundance.*
    —Wendell Berry, quoted in *Living the Sabbath*

I've worked at a variety of jobs in my life: coffee shop,
book-keeping, drive-thru window. I've emptied garbage
bins and mopped floors, chopped onions and done
payroll. With each job my respect grew for all that's required
to keep the world turning, as did my understanding of which
type of work suits me best. Nightshift was especially eye-open-

ing. Working all night and sleeping in the day sounded feasible
(and rather exotic), but staying awake all night does awful
things to a person. I left that job with a hearty appreciation for
the rhythms of day and night, gratefully rejoining the majority
of the world in its habits of sleeping and waking.

Another rhythm built into life that offers structure and rest
is the Sabbath[1]. Sabbath is a day of religious observance,
practiced by Jews from Friday night to Saturday night and by
most Christians on Sunday. Both of these faith traditions trace
the Sabbath to the biblical story of creation, where God
Himself rests from His labour on the seventh day. Later on, in
the accounts of Exodus and Deuteronomy, God commands
His people to work for six days and rest on the seventh.[2] The
seventh day is to be set apart, different from the others: a day
to rest and worship. To modern ears, the idea of Sabbath
sounds limiting and restrictive; but to the original audience,
this command would have shocked them with its radical
generosity. For four hundred years the people of Israel had
lived as slaves; a commandment to rest was an extravagant
gift.

We don't have slave-drivers forcing us to work around the
clock anymore, yet we live crazed and frantic lives, pressured
by demands to accomplish and achieve. Dedicating one day a
week to rest and worship rings of idleness and indulgence.
After all, who has time for rest? Time off is for vacation.
Saturdays will be too busy if I don't work on Sunday. Why
would I limit my schedule like that? When will I have time to
mow the lawn?

The idea of practicing Sabbath may sound strange to
those who don't observe it, and it's a hard sell in our current
climate. Most of us resist limits and constraints. We want flexibility and options, not structure and routine. But how has life
with unlimited freedom been working for you? Has this

approach brought the peace and rest you hope for? Maybe there's something to glean from the gift of Sabbath and those who have practiced it for thousands of years.

Counter-intuitively, having too much of a good thing can decrease our ability to enjoy it. Picture a buffet table where none of the food looks good, or hours of channel surfing to find a good film. Sometimes fewer options lead to greater appreciation. Limits and constraints, structure and tradition, can increase our enjoyment. The celebrations of Christmas and birthdays and weddings are sweetened and flavoured by our anticipation and waiting. Sabbath taps into this same dynamic.

Many of us are confused about what we really want and need. We long for peace and quiet, but our lives are packed with motion and noise and hurry. We want love and belonging, but pursuit of possessions and success gets in the way. Sabbath presents a different approach. Sabbath helps us order our lives in a different way. For one day a week we can pause from our activity, slow down, limit our options, and savour what we have. On Sunday we put limits around what we do: turn off the phone, postpone the housework, unplug the screens, and enjoy the day. We refrain from buying and spending and scrolling and liking, and we find other ways to interact with the world.

Once a week, whether I'm in the mood or not, I'm learning to rest, chill out, and shift my focus away from what has me stressed. On Sabbath I remember God as Creator, giver of life and beauty. I gaze on His gifts and slow down to let them sink in. Sabbath reminds me that I exist to receive love. My primary identity is not slave or worker, but beloved daughter, free from the tyranny of labour and striving. It feels good to work hard for six days, and there's satisfaction in what I can accomplish and produce; but Sabbath reminds me that

God is ultimately the one who sustains and upholds the world. Mark Buchanan's encouragement, "Cease what is necessary and embrace that which gives life," points me in the right direction. Sabbath invites me to take rest and refreshment seriously. Sabbath's not punishment, or an obligation to follow in fear. Sabbath's a reward for the week's work—something to look forward to. These days on Sunday, I choose activities that allow me to connect with God and others. I plan ahead: shopping for food, making arrangements with people I want to see, or thinking about the week to come. When the weather's nice, I get outside. I look at and listen to beautiful things. I talk about what I'm grateful for and give my attention to the people I'm with. Sabbath slows time down and trains me to be grateful for what I have today. Whatever I don't have can wait until Monday.

Every week Sabbath reminds me I'm part of God's story of life and new creation. As a Christian, I celebrate the resurrected and living Christ and remember His love, His example, and His power, which is making all things new.[3] Death and brokenness will not have the final word. There is more to the story than we see now. As I tell myself this story, and as I live it out through rest and recreation, I get a taste of the world to come. Sabbath tells me that I'm part of something bigger, and as I soak up the gifts offered to me, I'm better able to live with joy and hope and energy.

Acknowledgments

Thank you, Bobbie Hamm and Lee Stockburger, for your encouragement and prayers from the early days of this project and through its many, many variations.

Thank you, Cindy Hunt, for your feedback, perspective, and ideating, and for believing I have a message worthy to be heard. I'm so grateful to have you as a confessor.

Thank you, Karen Murdarasi, for all the coffee chats about writing, publishing, and not giving up on projects.

Thank you, Kay Ben-Avraham, for being an amazing editor, for coaching me, for helping when I got stuck, and for believing this project was worthwhile.

Notes

Introduction

1. 2 Peter 3:8-9 (NASB). "But do not let this one fact escape your notice, beloved, that with the Lord one day is like a thousand years, and a thousand years like one day. The Lord is not slow about His promise, as some count slowness, but is patient toward you, not wishing for any to perish but for all to come to repentance."

1. The Gift of Being More Than One Thing

1. Thank you, Matt Rawlins, for introducing the gifted/limited/broken framework as a way to look at myself and others.
2. The StrengthsFinder assessment was introduced in 2001 in the book *Now, Discover Your Strengths*, and has since been adapted to *CliftonStrengths*.
3. To learn more about CliftonStrengths and to take this assessment visit gallup.com.
4. A wonderful TED talk relevant to this topic is called "How to get better at the things you care about," by Eduardo Briceño:
   https://www.ted.com/talks/
   eduardo_briceno_how_to_get_better_at_the_things_you_care_about/
   footnotes?referrer=playlist-
   the_most_actionable_ted_talks&language=en
5. Michael Yaconelli, *Messy Spirituality*.

2. The Gift of Being & Becoming

1. To illustrate how uniquely each person has been created, consider this fact: the designers of the CliftonStrenths assessment report the chances of someone else having your top five strengths in your same order as… *1 in 33 million!* Check out gallupstrengthscenter.com to learn more.
2. "Vocation does not mean a goal that I pursue. It means a calling that I hear. Before I can tell my life what I want to do with it, I must listen to my life telling me who I am." *Let Your Life Speak: Listening for the Voice of Vocation*, by Parker J. Palmer. This small book looks at the journey of discovering who you are.

3. Ephesians 2:10 (NASB) refers to humanity as God's *masterpiece*. In Greek, the word is *poiema*. "For we are His workmanship, created in Christ Jesus for good works, which God prepared beforehand so that we would walk in them."

4. 1 Corinthians 4:7 (NASB), "For who regards you as superior? What do you have that you did not receive? And if you did receive it, why do you boast as if you had not received it?"

5. Two of my favourite books about discovering your vocation and learning to truly be yourself are *The Gift of Being Yourself*, by David G. Benner, and *Let Your Life Speak*, by Parker J. Palmer.

3. The Gift of Leading Yourself

1. Palmer, *Let Your Life Speak*.

2. John 10:10 (NASB), "The thief comes only to steal and kill and destroy; I came that they may have life, and have it abundantly."

5. The Gift of Changing Your Mind

1. Malcolm Gladwell writes extensively about decision-making in his book *Blink: The Power of Thinking Without Thinking*.

6. The Gift of Emotions

1. Thanks for this, Robin Dublin. I've never forgotten it.

2. Check out Susan David's TED talk, "The gift and power of emotional courage":   https://www.ted.com/talks/susan_david_the_gift_and_power_of_emotional_courage

3. One activity I've found helpful is to google a list of emotions and then spend some time recalling the last time I felt each of them. I noticed there were some emotions I was very familiar with and some I resisted. I wonder what you will notice?

7. The Gift of Attraction

1. I heard the concept of the "attraction gift" from Dean Sherman, author of *Relationships: The Key to Love, Sex, and Everything Else*.

8. The Gift of Creativity

1. A great book about the topic of creativity is *A Million Little Ways: Uncover the Art You Were Made to Live*, by Emily P. Freeman.
2. Skye Jethani develops the framework of "beauty, order and abundance" in many of his online sermons and messages and in his book *Futureville: Discover Your Purpose for Today by Reimagining Tomorrow*.

11. The Gift of a Should-Free Life

1. Thank you, Sharon Codd, for many great conversations, including the idea of removing *should* from my vocabulary.

12. The Gift of Leaving Your Comfort Zone

1. Genesis 12:1-3 (The Message), "God told Abram: 'Leave your country, your family, and your father's home for a land that I will show you.
    I'll make you a great nation
        and bless you.
    I'll make you famous;
        you'll be a blessing.
    I'll bless those who bless you;
        those who curse you I'll curse.
    All the families of the Earth
        will be blessed through you.'"

14. The Gift of Challenging Situations

1. From *Connecting: Healing Ourselves and Our Relationships*, by Larry Crabb.
2. 2 Corinthians 1:3-4 (NASB), "Blessed be the God and Father of our Lord Jesus Christ, the Father of mercies and God of all comfort, who comforts us in all our affliction so that we will be able to comfort those who are in any affliction with the comfort with which we ourselves are comforted by God."

16. The Gift of Taking Up A Hobby

1. Thank you, Cory Stroud, for your ongoing encouragement to "be interesting"!

17. The Gift of Being Present

1. A fantastic book that explores this theme in greater depth is Shauna Niequist's *Present Over Perfect: Leaving Behind Frantic for a Simple, More Soulful Way of Living*.
2. From *The Lost Art of Listening*, by Michael P. Nichols.

18. The Gift of Gratitude

1. A helpful book about how to cultivate an attitude of gratefulness is *One Thousand Gifts: A Dare to Live Fully Right Where You Are*, by Ann Voskamp. Her blog is excellent, too: annvoskamp.com.

21. The Gift of Intentional Friendship

1. A great book that looks at various types of relationships, including friendship, is *The Four Loves*, by C. S. Lewis. Check out this quote: "Friendship… is born at the moment when one man says to another 'What! You too? I thought that no one but myself…'"

22. The Gift of Confession

1. The books *Celebration of Discipline: The Path to Spiritual Growth* by Richard Foster, and *The Life You've Always Wanted: Spiritual Disciplines for Ordinary People* by John Ortberg, both talk about the discipline of confession.
2. When it comes to the discipline of confession and staying connected to others, here are some questions to consider:
   - With whom do you talk about your struggles?
   - Who knows about and celebrates your victories?
   - Who acts as a sounding board when you need to make important decisions?
   - With whom do you have healthy fun?
   - Where do you find role models to inspire your faith and life?

23. The Gift of Knowing What Story You're In

1. Donald Miller explains how a good story involves a character who wants something and has to overcome obstacles to get it in *A Million Miles in a Thousand Years: How I Learned to Live a Better Story*.

2. By *story* I don't mean fictional or not absolutely real and true. *Story* refers to a framework of looking at life and reality, a type of perspective that makes sense of all the elements and aspects of life—what we see and don't see, what we are in control of and what we aren't, what has happened before us, what is going on this moment, and what is still to come.

3. Ephesians 1:11-12 (The Message), "It's in Christ that we find out who we are and what we are living for. Long before we first heard of Christ and got our hopes up, he had his eye on us, had designs on us for glorious living, part of the overall purpose he is working out in everything and everyone."

4. Colossians 1:16-17 (NASB), "For by Him all things were created, both in the heavens and on earth, visible and invisible, whether thrones or dominions or rulers or authorities—all things have been created through Him and for Him. He is before all things, and in Him all things hold together." And John 1:1-3 (NASB), "In the beginning was the Word, and the Word was with God, and the Word was God. He was in the beginning with God. All things came into being through Him, and apart from Him nothing came into being that has come into being."

24. The Gift of Reflecting on God's Image

1. You can learn about Malala Yousafzai by reading her autobiography *I am Malala: The Story of the Girl Who Stood Up for Education and was Shot by the Taliban,* by Malala Yousafzai and Christina Lamb.

2. A great video about what it means to be God's image bearer is The Bible Project's video, "The Image of God." https://thebibleproject. com/explore/image-god/

3. A great verse about following and learning from others is 1 Corinthians 11:1 (NIV), "Follow my example, as I follow the example of Christ."

26. The Gift of Sabbath

1. To read more about Sabbath, and other spiritual disciplines, check out *Mudhouse Sabbath: An Invitation to a Life of Spiritual Discipline,* by Lauren Winner.

2. Commands regarding the Sabbath are given in Exodus 20 and Deuteronomy 5, as well as other places in the Old Testament.

3. Revelation 21:3-5 (NASB) gives a picture of what's to come and speaks of God's intention to restore all of creation, setting the world right: "And I heard a loud voice from the throne saying, 'Look! God's

dwelling place is now among the people, and he will dwell with them. They will be his people, and God himself will be with them and be their God. He will wipe every tear from their eyes. There will be no more death or mourning or crying or pain, for the old order of things has passed away.' He who was seated on the throne said, 'I am making everything new!' Then he said, 'Write this down, for these words are trustworthy and true.'"

Made in the USA
Monee, IL
23 June 2023